491
W 164

IUNCTURA CALLIDUS ACRI

IUNCTURA CALLIDUS ACRI:
A STUDY OF
PERSIUS' SATIRES

CYNTHIA S. DESSEN

ILLINOIS STUDIES IN LANGUAGE AND LITERATURE

59

UNIVERSITY OF ILLINOIS PRESS   URBANA, CHICAGO, AND LONDON   1968

"verba togae sequeris, iunctura callidus acri . . ."
Persius, *Sat.*, V.14
"the most heterogeneous ideas . . . yoked by violence together."
Samuel Johnson, *Life of Cowley*

PREFACE

When I was searching for a dissertation topic in 1963 I became interested in Persius because he was a difficult writer who seemed to be either disliked or ignored by most classicists. Professor W. S. Anderson was an exception and the interesting results of his analysis of Satire V (*Philol. Quart.* 39 [1960], pp. 66–81) encouraged me to apply his methods to the other Satires. Originally this study was a close critical reading of these poems for the classicist with a knowledge of Persius, and in its present form it will probably still appeal primarily to the specialist. Since it is the first extended study of Persius in English, however, I have omitted or abbreviated much of the original discussion of the scholarship on Persius and I have provided translations of most of the quotes and longer phrases in other languages. These translations are not meant to be poetic or even artistic; they are intended to clarify my readings of the Satires and they often reflect my own interpretation of a passage. I have also removed most of the scholarship on the Greek antecedents of Satire IV to the Appendix to save the general reader the trouble of wading through it. Even so it is only a brief survey of a large body of material; I limited myself to those items relevant to the fourth Satire and I did not attempt to offer any new evidence.

The title of this study, *Iunctura Callidus Acri,* is a compliment which Persius' teacher, Cornutus, pays his pupil in the fifth Satire. Echoing Horace's remark that the poet will succeed "if a skillful juxtaposition [lit. joining] makes an old word seem new" (*notum si callida verbum reddiderit iunctura novum, Ars Poet.,* 47–48), Persius characteristically changes Horace's words and thought slightly to produce a different idea which still recalls the original. Thus he describes himself literally as "skillful at the sharp juxtaposition." This phrase, I think, refers to his peculiar use of metaphor, whereby he boldly unites very disparate ideas to shock his

vii

reader into a new perspective. An example of this is the controlling metaphor of Satire IV which equates the politician with the male prostitute. I have analyzed this technique at greater length in my discussion of individual Satires; it is so characteristic of Persius' manner of thought that the phrase which he uses to describe it seemed an appropriate title for a study of his poems. Samuel Johnson echoes Persius when he characterizes the subject matter of the metaphysical poets as "the most heterogeneous ideas . . . yoked by violence together." Perhaps it was this quality in Persius' work which appealed to one of these poets who imitated him, John Donne.

For their support and encouragement of the completion of this study I am deeply indebted to both the Woodrow Wilson Foundation and to my thesis director, Professor Henry T. Rowell. I am grateful also to Professor John J. Bateman of the University of Illinois, who suggested many helpful revisions prior to publication.

CONTENTS

CHAPTER ONE

THE RHETORICAL AND POETIC BACKGROUND OF THE SATIRES

Of all the Roman satirists Persius has received the least recognition from classical scholars, yet in his own lifetime and throughout the Middle Ages he was admired both as a poet and as a moralist. According to the anonymous author of Persius' *Vita*, Lucan praised the poetic technique of his close friend and fellow Stoic:

Sed Lucanus mirabatur adeo scripta Flacci, ut vix se retineret recitantem a clamore: quae illius essent vera esse poemata, se ludos facere.[1]

Lucan thought so highly of Flaccus' compositions that when reciting them he could scarcely keep from proclaiming that these were true poems, while his own were mere trifles.

Martial and Quintilian also mention Persius but their praise is more restrained. To Martial Persius exemplifies the virtues of publishing rarely: *saepius in libro numeratur Persius uno / quam levis in tota Marsus Amazonide* (Persius is more esteemed for his single volume than worthless Marsus for his whole *Amazonid*, IV.29.7–8), and Quintilian includes Persius among the poets whom he urges the young orator to study, commenting that *multum et verae gloriae quamvis uno libro Persius meruit* (although he wrote only one book, Persius has earned much well-deserved fame, X.1.94). Although one may question whether Martial and Quintilian admired Persius themselves, their words imply that his reputation was already well established soon after his death.

---

[1] The text is that of Wendell V. Clausen, ed., *A. Persi Flacci Saturarum Liber* (Oxford, 1956), p. 38, based on the suggestions of S. G. Owen, ed., *A. Persi Flacci et D. Iuni Iuvenalis Saturae* (2nd ed., Oxford, 1949), pp. xiv–xv: *Sed Lucanus mirabatur adeo scripta Flacci, ut vix se retineret recitante eo de more quin illa esse vera poemata, sua ludos diceret.*

1

In late antiquity and the Middle Ages Persius' Stoicism assured him a place in the writings of the leading theologians. Lactantius, Jerome, Augustine, and Isidore all quote him extensively and later he appears in the works of a number of writers, including Gunzo of Novara, Luitprand of Cremona, and John of Salisbury.[2] Furthermore, the majority of manuscripts for the Satires are early rather than late, an unusual occurrence among classical authors. Of the fifty-nine manuscripts which Clausen lists in his 1956 edition of Persius, twenty-five are dated in the ninth to tenth centuries, eighteen in the tenth to eleventh centuries, twelve in the eleventh to twelfth centuries, and only four in the thirteenth to fifteenth centuries.[3]

The first edition of the Satires was published at Rome in 1469 or 1470 by Ulrich Han. The Satires of Juvenal were not included in this edition although they are occasionally bound with it in existing copies. Following the *editio princeps* there were one or more new editions every year, several of which included Juvenal's poems and/or printed the prologue as the first Satire. In 1477 Bartholomew Fontius wrote the first commentary on the Satires; this was published separately and then added to the text in 1480. A year later Giovanni Brittanico published a second commentary which was combined with the text in the 1486 edition printed at Brescia. In 1499 the scholia, attributed to Cornutus, were published and in 1544 the first modern language translation appeared, that of Abel Foulon in French. An Italian translation by Giovanni Vallone followed in 1576, but the Satires did not appear in English until Barton Holyday translated them in 1616. Thus the early English imitators of Persius, such as John Donne (*Satires, ca.* 1593–1597), Joseph Hall (*Virgidemiarum*, 1597–1598), and John Marston (*The Scourge of Villanie*, 1598), undoubtedly read a Latin edition of his works.

In 1605 Isaac Casaubon published his edition of the Satires prefaced by a vigorous defense of Persius. Casaubon praised Persius' Stoic earnestness and philosophic constancy over Horace's eclecti-

---

[2] M. Manitius, "Beiträge zur Geschichte römischer Dichter im Mittelalter," *Philologus* 47 (1888): pp. 710–720, gives an extensive list of references to Persius by writers of the third through the fourteenth centuries. For a list of manuscripts to 1300, see the same author's "Philologisches aus alten Bibliothekskatalogen (bis 1300)," *Rhein. Mus.* 47 (1892): Suppl. pp. 52–54.

[3] Clausen (ed. 1956), pp. vii–xv, 40–41. There is also the famous palimpsest from Bobbio, Vaticanus 5750 (*Bob.*), dated in the sixth century. In his review of Clausen's edition in *Gnomon* 32 (1960): p. 120, O. Seel, using slightly different figures, arrives at the same conclusion.

cism, but as Dryden later remarked, "neither Casaubon himself, nor any for him, can defend his numbers, or the purity of his Latin. Casaubon gives this point for lost, and pretends not to justify either the measures or the words of Persius; he is evidently beneath Horace and Juvenal in both." [4]

Both Julius Caesar Scaliger, with whom Casaubon debated Persius' merits, and later Dryden argued that the obscurity of the Satires outweighed their ethical value; this shift in interest during the sixteenth and seventeenth centuries from content to technique marks the beginning of Persius' decline in popularity.[5] Dryden is particularly harsh on Persius' style: ". . . his verse is scabrous, and hobbling . . . his diction is hard, his figures are too bold and daring, and his tropes, particularly his metaphors, insufferably strained." [6]

Fifty years later one of Persius' translators, Edmund Burton, argued: " 'Tis rather owing to *want of assiduity in the reader* than to *want of perspicuity in the Author,* that Persius is deemed an obscure, inelegant, and unintelligible writer. . . . The only requisites that seem necessary, towards attaining a right understanding of Persius, are a close attention to the stile, a perfect acquaintance with customs, times, and places, and, above all, a firm resolution to surpass every vincible opposition." [7] Unfortunately many later readers have lacked this "firm resolution" and dismissed Persius summarily. Rudolf Hirzel criticizes his "ponderous disposition" and adds, "his expression is affected and obscure." [8] Nicola Terzaghi finds Persius "resentful and gloomy" and labels Lucan's praise for his poems immature and overly enthusiastic.[9] Even one of his more sympathetic critics, E. C. Witke, says, "He could not

[4] John Dryden, "A Discourse Concerning the Original and Progress of Satire" (London, 1693), reprinted in *Essays of John Dryden*, ed. W. P. Ker (New York, 1961) 2: p. 70.

[5] Cf. J. C. Scaliger, *Poetices Libri Septem* (Lyon, 1561), VI.6:

Persii vero stilus morosus et ille ineptus, qui cum legi vellet quae scripsisset, intellegi noluit quae legerentur. quanquam nunc a nobis omnia intelliguntur. at fuit tempus, cum inter ignota haberetur. illum igitur mittamus.

In truth Persius' style is morose and he himself inept, because although he wanted people to read his writings, he did not want them to understand what they read. Now, however, we understand all his works; but there was a time when he was unknown. Therefore let us dismiss him.

[6] Dryden, p. 70.

[7] Edmund Burton, tr., *The Satyrs of Persius* (London, 1752), p. iii.

[8] Rudolf Hirzel, *Der Dialog* (Leipzig, 1895) 2: p. 35.

[9] Nicola Terzaghi, "Satire e poesia nella letteratura latina," *Annali della scuola normale superiore di Pisa,* Cl. di lett. 12 (1943): p. 108.

take over the Horatian smile, and hence replaced by mechanical devices, intellectualized obscurity, and puzzles and *tours de force* what he could not afford to represent emotionally, sympathetically, and with a delightful realism rooted in the creatural and the everyday." [10]

Despite this general distaste for Persius, several scholars have studied his works. Villeneuve's *Essai sur Perse* (Paris, 1918) remains the standard work on all aspects of the Satires although it suffers occasionally from the author's fondness for biographical conjecture.[11] In a more recent study Enzo Marmorale contends that Persius was a serious poet but he does not support his thesis with a close critical analysis of the Satires.[12] Those who have written shorter works on Persius have usually confined themselves to discussions of his Stoicism, his peculiar language, and his relationship to Horace.[13] Only recently have critics such as W. S. Anderson, E. C. Witke, and Kenneth Reckford examined Persius' poetic technique, yet even their investigations have been limited in scope.[14]

The traditional scholarly prejudice toward Persius perhaps originates in the rather colorless portrait of him given in the *Vita* appended to the Satires. From its subtitle in several of the manuscripts, *De commentario Probi Valeri sublata* (excerpted from the commentary of Valerius Probus), this *Vita* has acquired additional

[10] Edward C. Witke, *Latin Satire: The Classical Genre and its Medieval Development* (Diss., Harvard University, 1961), p. 92.

[11] Villeneuve, for example, attributes Persius' lack of humor to his Etruscan ancestry because he believes that the tomb paintings reveal the somber nature of these people (pp. 3–4). He also offers several unfounded conjectures, such as his description of Persius' life: "Thus his brief life passed, with no significant events and with no other interests than the love of literature, philosophy, and virtue, yet embellished with gentle affections and strong friendships" (p. 108).

[12] Enzo Marmorale, *Persio* (2nd ed., Florence, 1956).

[13] On Persius' Stoicism see C. Burnier, *Le Rôle des satires de Perse dans le développement du néo-stoïcisme* (Chaux-de-Fonds, 1909); N. Festa, "Persio e Cleante," *Scritti per il XIX centenario dalla nascità di Persio* (Volterra, 1936): pp. 15–30; and J. Martin, "Persius, Poet of the Stoics," *Greece and Rome* 8 (1939): pp. 172–182. Persius' language has been analyzed by T. Ciresola, *La formazione del linguaggio poetico di Persio* (Rovereto, 1953), and G. Faranda, "Caratteristiche dello stile e del linguaggio poetico di Persio," *Rendic. del Istit. Lombardo*, Cl. di lett. 88 (1955): pp. 512–538. D. Henss, "Die Imitationstechnik des Persius," *Philologus* 99 (1955): pp. 277–294, offers some interesting comments on Persius' relationship to Horace.

[14] William S. Anderson, "Part Versus Whole in Persius' Fifth Satire," *Philol. Quart.* 39 (1960): pp. 66–81; Edward C. Witke, "The Function of Persius' Choliambics," *Mnemosyne* 4, 15 (1962): pp. 153–158; and Kenneth J. Reckford, "Studies in Persius," *Hermes* 90 (1962): pp. 476–504. Reckford comments on certain images in each Satire but he does not discuss any poem in detail.

authority as a document of the first century A.D. There is no firm evidence, however, that Probus ever wrote a commentary to the Satires, and the form and style of the *Vita* are too anonymous to identify its author or its date.[15] The *Vita* describes Persius as an aristocratic Stoic intellectual who lost his father and stepfather as a child and presumably grew up in the company of his mother and aunts. The references to his philosophic pursuits, his interest in books, and his poor health suggest that he was a studious youth out of touch with the world. The brief summary of his character strengthens this impression:

fuit morum lenissimorum, verecundiae virginalis, famae pulchrae, pietatis erga matrem et sororem et amitam exemplo sufficientis. fuit frugi, pudicus.[16]

he was a most gentle person, of maidenly modesty, with a fine reputation and noteworthy in his affection for his mother, sister, and aunt. He was frugal and chaste.

To many critics Persius' poetic style corroborates this picture. They cite the numerous echoes of earlier writers in his work as evidence that he spent most of his time closeted in his library and they conclude that this withdrawal from life explains his predilection for obscure conceits.[17] To strengthen their argument these critics usually mention the few passages in the Satires which seem to substantiate the facts given in the *Vita*. Persius' scornful question to the man who boasts of his Etruscan ancestry, *an deceat pulmonem rumpere ventis / stemmate quod Tusco ramum millesime ducis?* (is it fitting to burst your lungs with hot air because you are the thousandth sprout on a Tuscan family tree? III.27–28), and his reference to the Tyrrhenian sea as *meum mare*

[15] A. Rostagni, *Suetonio de Poetis e biografi minori* (Turin, 1944), pp. 167–176, attributes the biography to Probus who, he argues, would have possessed the detailed knowledge of Persius' life and the interest in the textual history of the Satires manifested by the author of the *Vita*. Vincenzo Ciaffi, *Introduzione a Persio* (Turin, 1942), pp. 3–10, shares Rostagni's views whereas Riccardo Scarcia, "Osservazioni critiche. IV. A proposito della *Vita* di Persio," *Riv. di cult. class. e medioev.* 6 (1964): pp. 298–302, regards the *Vita* as a compilation of the fourth century modeled on Donatus' life of Vergil.

[16] Rostagni, p. 173, suggests that the author of the *Vita* emphasizes Persius' gentle character to counteract the impression gained from the Satires that he was rebelling against his society. If Persius' audience was familiar with the device of the satiric persona, however (cf. *infra*, pp. 7–9), they would not have made this identification.

[17] Cf. M. Schanz and C. Hosius, *Geschichte der römischen Literatur*, Müllers Handbuch, 7, 1³ (4th ed., Munich, 1935) 2: p. 480; E. Paratore, *Storia della letteratura latina* (Florence, 1951), pp. 591–592; and J. W. Duff, *A Literary History of Rome in the Silver Age* (2nd ed., London, 1960), p. 233.

(my sea, VI.7), recall his own Etruscan lineage, while his childhood is vividly remembered in the well-known scene from the third Satire:

> Saepe oculos, memini, tangebam parvus olivo,
> grandia si nollem morituri verba Catonis
> discere non sano multum laudanda magistro,
> quae pater adductis sudans audiret amicis [44–47].[18]

Often as a child, I remember, I used to dab my eyes with olive oil to avoid learning Cato's solemn death speech (much admired by my mad teacher), which my father, in a cold sweat, would drag his friends to hear me recite.

This evaluation of Persius rests upon the biographical interpretation of literature which Wilamowitz enthusiastically endorsed in the early part of this century. In his study, *Platon* (Berlin, 1920), he stated: "The philologist is, to be sure, an interpreter, but not merely an interpreter of words, for he will never understand these if he does not understand the soul from which they spring. He must also be the interpreter of this soul. Since the entire art of biography, therefore, rests in interpretation, it is actually the work of the philologist raised to a higher power. Thus the problem consists simply in understanding how this man came to be, what he wished, thought, and accomplished." [19] Classicists have found the biographical approach particularly useful because it allows them to include literary works among the relatively meager sources of information on classical civilization. This approach assumes, of course, that these works reflect this civilization fairly accurately, and in the case of satire the satirists' insistence upon their honesty would appear to confirm this assumption. During the past twenty years, however, several critics of English literature have emphasized the rhetorical aspects of formal English satire and their findings cast doubt upon the usefulness of interpreting satire solely from the factual and biographical points of view.[20]

---

[18] Marmorale, pp. 111–113, Villeneuve (1918a), p. 3.

[19] Ulrich von Wilamowitz-Moellendorff, *Platon* (2 v., 2nd ed., Berlin, 1920) 1: p. 4. Harold Cherniss, "The Biographical Fashion in Literary Criticism," *Univ. Calif. Pub. in Class. Phil.* 12 (1933–1944): p. 283 ff., translates this passage and attacks its premises rather harshly. Cherniss' remarks, which were undoubtedly inspired by the rise of New Criticism, are dated in regard to English literature but still pertinent to classical studies.

[20] There is a great deal of literature on this subject. M. C. Randolph contributed two pioneer studies, *The Neo-Classic Theory of the Formal Verse Satire in England, 1700–1750* (Diss., Univ. of North Carolina, 1939), and "The Structural Design of the Formal Verse Satire," *Philol. Quart.* 21 (1942): pp. 368–384. Among the more recent scholarship, the most valuable works

These critics point out that although most satirists profess to speak simply and sincerely, this is in part a rhetorical convention introduced to gain the listener's goodwill; in practice the satirist, like the orator, often wins his point by the skillful blending of truth and fiction. One of the most common satiric devices is the persona, or invented character, through which the author speaks. The persona may be a character clearly distinct from the author, such as Encolpius in the *Satyricon* or Naevolus in Juvenal's ninth Satire. These figures reveal the vices of others and are themselves satirized by the author. A more complex example of this speaker is the ironic persona perfected by Swift in such characters as Gulliver or the projector of *A Modest Proposal*. Finally, the author may use a first person persona, as does Horace in many of his Satires and Pope in his *Epistle to Dr. Arbuthnot*. Here the author is not satirizing himself, but is attempting to persuade his audience that his moral credentials qualify him to hold up his own life as a virtuous example and to pass judgment on others. While it seems difficult, in this case, to distinguish the author from his persona, the latter often manifests itself in contradictory character traits and stock arguments.

In Pope's satire Maynard Mack distinguishes three personae, the *vir bonus,* the naive man or *ingenu,* and the satiric hero warring against evil.[21] Alvin Kernan devotes the first chapter of his study of Renaissance satire to a general analysis of this last type and many of his comments on the Renaissance form of this persona apply equally well to Persius and Juvenal. Using the term "satirist" to refer to the satiric persona, Kernan illustrates the artificial nature of this "satirist" by pointing out the conflicts between his public

---

include M. Mack, "The Muse of Satire," *Yale Review* 41 (1951): pp. 80–92; W. B. Ewald, *The Masks of Jonathan Swift* (Oxford, 1954); A. Kernan, *The Cankered Muse: Satire of the English Renaissance* (New Haven, 1959); and J. Aden, "Pope and the Satiric Adversary," *Stud. in Eng. Lit.* 2 (1962): pp. 267–286. It should be pointed out that the term *persona,* which these critics discuss, does not have the same meaning in Latin rhetorical theory which it does when applied to formal English satire. From its original meaning of "dramatic mask" this term was extended to mean "a dramatic character" and eventually "a person." In rhetorical literature it is also used to translate the Greek *ēthos* and refers to the personality projected by the orator to persuade his audience to accept his arguments. There is abundant evidence, I believe, in Latin poetry to prove that the poets, including the satirists, adopted this device; but the rhetoricians seldom use the term *persona* in this way when they discuss literature, and it is a moot point whether their rhetorical theory recognized this device in poetry.

[21] Mack, pp. 88–91.

and private personality. As part of his public personality the "satirist" emphasizes his candor, his simple style, and his unpretentious background. His moral code confirms his character, for he endorses all the stock virtues of honesty, industry, integrity, and simplicity.[22] Believing that he is the only rational being left in an irrational world, he feels forced to write satire and shows little tolerance or humor toward mankind's foibles.

The private personality of this "satirist" is much more disturbing. He claims to describe the world as it is but actually distorts it greatly, and although he says that he despises evil, the vigor and passion of his descriptions betray a morbid fascination with perversity. Furthermore, in attacking those who are enslaved to their emotions he often loses control of his own.[23] These contradictions in character lead Kernan to conclude that the "satirist" must be regarded as but one poetic device used by the author to express his poetic vision, a device which can be dispensed with or varied to suit his purposes." [24]

The persona is no longer a novel concept in English literary criticism. Few critics would agree with Ehrenpreis that the persona has no place in formal satire, but many still maintain quite rightly that the satirist's own experience and feelings shape his persona.[25] In classical studies, however, this concept has only recently been acknowledged, primarily in research on the elegiac poets.[26] As

[22] It is interesting to compare this description of the "satirist" with Antonius' remarks on the proper character for defendants in a lawsuit (Cicero, de Or., II.43.184):

> Horum igitur exprimere mores oratione iustos, integros, religiosos, timidos, perferentes iniuriarum, mirum quiddam valet.

> It is very effective, therefore, to portray these people in your speech as just, upright, pious, and timid souls suffering injustice.

Although the "satirist" may be more outspoken than the defendant, the character of each is artfully contrived.

[23] Kernan, pp. 15–26.

[24] Ibid., p. 15.

[25] I. Ehrenpreis, "Personae," Restoration and Eighteenth Century Literature: Essays in Honor of Alan Dugald McKillop, ed. C. Camden (Chicago, 1963): pp. 25–37. Ehrenpreis acknowledges the value of the "ironical persona," but he sees even this character as a spokesman for the real author; hence he believes that "A Modest Proposal makes sense only if we treat the voice as the author's throughout" (p. 35). Ehrenpreis' article prompted a lively symposium on "The Concept of the Persona in Satire," Satire Newsletter 3 (Spring, 1966): pp. 89–153. Most of the participants disagreed with Ehrenpreis' extreme views but noted that there is seldom a complete dichotomy between the poet and his persona.

[26] Cf. A. W. Allen, " 'Sincerity' and the Roman Elegists," Class. Phil. 45 (1950): pp. 145–160, and R. M. Durling, "Ovid as Praeceptor Amoris," Class.

early as 1961 W. S. Anderson remarked: "Satire, which is equally Roman and personal, has so far failed to share the benefits of this critical concept. We know that all Romans who engaged in literary pursuits, by the end of the second century B.C., studied rhetorical principles consistently in their formative years; but scholars have found it easier to grasp the elegist's use of a persona than they have the satirist's." [27] Anderson has continued to press for the validity of the persona, supporting his arguments with studies of this device in Horace and Juvenal; he has also made several suggestions concerning Persius' persona, and Witke has treated its development in his analysis of the prologue.[28] The present study continues these investigations, considering the different personae of individual Satires as well as the related rhetorical device of the imaginary adversary.

Mere rhetorical analysis of the figures peculiar to satire will not

---

Journal 53 (1957–1958): pp. 157–167, as well as his more recent discussion of the personae of Horace and Ovid in *The Figure of the Poet in Renaissance Epic* (Cambridge, 1965), pp. 13–43.

[27] William S. Anderson, "Juvenal and Quintilian," *Yale Class. Stud.* 17 (1961): p. 26. The remarks of two recent reviewers of Kernan's book reveal the extent of the gap between modern criticism and classical studies. Ronald Paulson notes (*Jour. of Eng. and Ger. Philol.* 59 [1960]: p. 737): "Kernan's particular bugbear is the identification of the poet with his satiric persona, a confusion which one would think long since dead had it not appeared, flourishing, a few years ago in John Peter's *Satire and Complaint* [Oxford, 1956]." Kathleen Williams adds (*Mod. Lang. Notes* 76 [1961]: p. 346): "One may doubt whether it is now necessary to argue at much length the position that a satiric poem or play is a work of art like any other, and that the figure which gives voice to satiric comment differs to a greater or less degree from the actual author, who has created that figure for his own exact purposes." Nevertheless, the most recent work in Roman satire, N. Rudd, *The Satires of Horace* (Cambridge, 1966), disregards the possibility that Horace uses a persona.

[28] Witke (1962). Cf. Anderson (1961), p. 27: "The assumptions of Satires 1 and 5 that style does betray the essential man suggest that we should be careful in picturing the young Persius, on the basis of his writings, as an innocent bookish Stoic, much under the influence of women and his tutors, who spoke directly from his heart. . . . He, too, has assumed the part appropriate to his special type of satire." Anderson also notes that "Horace's and Persius' satiric personae do not conflict with the moral implications of their poetry, and the nice blending of the ironic and Stoic speakers with satiric themes attests to the care with which the persona has been created" (p. 28). Anderson discusses the general importance of the persona in "Roman Satirists and Literary Criticism," *Bucknell Review* 12, 3 (1964): pp. 106–113, and its specific application to Horace in "The Roman Socrates: Horace and His Satires," *Critical Essays on Roman Literature*, ed. J. P. Sullivan (London, 1963) 2: pp. 1–37, and to Juvenal in "Anger in Juvenal and Seneca," *Univ. Calif. Pub. in Class. Phil.* 19, 3 (1964): pp. 127–196.

suffice, however, for, as a well-known English critic has noted, "to recognize these figures is not to understand how they create satire, and it is to ignore how the details they classify do not function alone, but catch fire in their contexts. The texture of satire at its keenest is truly organic; its parts inter-relate; sometimes it approaches the richness and integration of a poem."[29] This is particularly true in regard to Persius, who considered himself a poet as well as a satirist. Horace may have denied (albeit facetiously) that satire was poetry and preferred to call his efforts *sermoni propiora* (closer to conversation, *Ser.*, I.4.42), but Persius considered his satire *carmen* worthy of being brought *ad sacra vatum* (to the shrines of the bards, *Prol.*, 7), and his skillful poetic technique leaves little doubt that he was fully aware of his artistic achievement. Although he claims to cultivate a simple style (*Sat.*, 5.19–20), Persius employs two devices associated with the elevated style of poetry, imagery and metaphor, in a characteristically poetic manner: the theme of the Satire is usually stated in a controlling metaphor and developed through a pattern of related images. To analyze Persius' metaphors we must turn to the techniques of modern criticism rather than those of classical rhetoric because the rhetoricians did not fully understand the poetic value of this device. From Aristotle to Quintilian they treat the metaphor as a word or phrase introduced to ornament a speech, involving a transfer from genus to species and vice-versa or from animate to inanimate objects and vice-versa. Hermogenes of Tarsus (*fl.* second century A.D.) alone seems to recognize the poetic role of metaphor:

Τροπή ἐστι τὸ μὴ ἐξ ὑποκειμένου πράγματος ἀλλοτρίου δὲ σημαντικὸν ὄνομα θεῖναι, κοινὸν εἶναι δυνάμενον καὶ τοῦ ὑποκειμένου κἀι τοῦ ἔξωθεν ἐμφαινομένου, ὃ καλεῖται καὶ μεταφορὰ παρὰ τοῖς γραμματικοῖς, οὐχ ὡς ἐκεῖνοι λέγουσι τὸ ἀπὸ τῶν ἀψύχων ἐπὶ τὰ ἔμψυχα, καὶ τὸ ἀνάπαλιν, καθόλου γὰρ ἡ ῥητορικὴ

---

[29] John Holloway, "The Well-Filled Dish: An Analysis of Swift's Satire," *Hudson Review* 9 (1956): p. 21. Cf. Quintilian, IX.3.100, on those who love rhetorical figures for their own sake:

> non desinant eas nectere quas sine substantia sectari tam est ridiculum quam quaerere habitum gestumque sine corpore.

> They cannot resist adding these figures to one another, even though it is as foolish to search for them without reference to one's subject matter as it is to consider dress and gesture apart from physical form.

Yet most of the ancient rhetoricians, including Quintilian, discuss figures out of context.

πολυπραγμονοῦσα μηδὲν μήτε ἐμψύχων μήτε ἀψύχων οὕτω χρῆται ἀλλοτρίοις ὀνόμασιν [*Inv.*, IV.10].[30]

A trope is the introduction of a word not related to the subject matter at hand, but signifying something extraneous, which simultaneously unites both the subject matter and this alien concept. This figure is also called a metaphor by the grammarians, but it does not involve a transfer, as they say, from inanimate to animate things and vice-versa; for rhetoric uses extraneous concepts in the manner described, and does not in general concern itself with animate and inanimate things.

While the earlier rhetoricians do not conceive of a metaphor as anything more than a single ornamental figure akin to the simile, they do discuss what we would call a controlling metaphor under the concept of *allegoria*. This term has a much broader meaning than our word "allegory"; according to Quintilian the figure *aut aliud verbis aliud sensu ostendit aut etiam interim contrarium* (says one thing and means another, often contrary, thing, VIII.6.44). Quintilian includes in this concept both simple ironic statements and pure allegory as we understand it; as an example of the latter he mentions Vergil's ninth Eclogue where within a pastoral setting Vergil appears as Menalcas. In addition, *allegoria* may be used throughout the poem, and it is here, as in Quintilian's example of Horace's "ship of state" Ode (I.14), that this figure most resembles the controlling metaphor. To the classical rhetoricians a poem whose meaning could not be understood from the literal sense of the words clearly seemed allegorical. Aside from Quintilian, most of these rhetoricians distrust this figure because it conflicts with their ideal of a lucid style; Aristotle dismisses it as a form of *ainigma* and Demetrius and Cicero both warn against the dangers of obscurity.[31] To the Stoics, however, *allegoria* was a natural poetic technique, as P. De Lacy points out: "The condemnation of poetry normally involves the assumption of a simple relation between the *phone* [words] of a poem and its meaning. Poems are interpreted literally, as if each word were used with the precision and clarity of a philosophic writing. The more usual Stoic view was that the poet does not mean literally what he says, but rather disguises his meaning by giving it poetic elaboration."[32]

[30] Quoted by W. B. Stanford, *Greek Metaphor* (Oxford, 1936), p. 14. Cf. also Louis Mackey, "Aristotle and Feidelson on Metaphor: Toward a Reconciliation of Ancient and Modern," *Arion* 4, 2 (1965): pp. 272–285.

[31] Aristotle, *Poet.*, XXII.4–6, Demetrius, *Eloc.*, II.99–102, Cicero, *de Or.*, III.42.167. Cf. *ad Her.*, IV.34.46.

[32] Philip De Lacy, "Stoic Views of Poetry," *Amer. Jour. of Philol.* 69 (1948): p. 226.

According to the Stoics *allegoria* rendered philosophy palatable to the unphilosophically minded. In addition they felt that certain elevated ideas required a more elaborate form of expression than prose. They therefore endorsed the poets' use of *allegoria* and based their theories of literary criticism upon it.[33]

From his study of Stoicism Persius probably learned the value of developing his satiric-philosophic themes through a controlling metaphor and related images. His use of metaphor is much more complex than the rhetorical concept of *allegoria,* but to a contemporary Stoic his Satires no doubt seemed allegorical in the classical sense because they did not always make literal sense. The controlling metaphor of the first Satire, for example, equates the poet and his poetry. Clearly Persius does not mean this literally, but this metaphorical equation allows him to prove that the effeminate, sensual poetry of his day reflects the effeminate, depraved character of contemporary poets.

W. S. Anderson's study of Horace's and Juvenal's metaphors provides a convenient framework for a discussion of this device in Persius.[34] Anderson points out that Horace selects common, unmetaphorical words, such as *servus* or *praecepta,* and by repeating them in different contexts and playing upon their literal and figurative meanings, he develops them into controlling metaphors. In Anderson's words, "he merges it [the controlling metaphor] with the dramatic framework of his Satire so skillfully that it possesses no immediate, but a cumulative, significance." [35] Juvenal, in contrast, chooses paradoxical metaphors which he exploits for their shock value, but he frequently diminishes their effectiveness by combining them with other rhetorical devices.[36] Persius occupies a position midway between these extremes. Like Horace he develops metaphors from simple words and he is apt to borrow a metaphor from another author (often Horace) and recast it in more literal terms.[37] But he often anticipates Juvenal's fault of introducing other rhetorical elements which obscure these metaphors.

---

[33] *Ibid.,* pp. 268–269. The extant writings of Persius' teacher, Cornutus, also indicate his interest in *allegoria.*

[34] William S. Anderson, "Imagery in the Satires of Horace and Juvenal," *Amer. Jour. of Philol.* 81 (1960): pp. 225–260.

[35] *Ibid.,* p. 228.

[36] *Ibid.,* pp. 246–247.

[37] Wolfgang Kugler, *Des Persius' Wille zu sprachlicher Gestaltung in seiner Wirkung auf Ausdruck und Komposition* (Diss., Berlin/Würzburg, 1940), thor-

The presence of a pattern of related images and metaphors entails another poetic device, verbal repetition. Even reading Persius' Satires rapidly one cannot help noticing the large number of repetitions in proportion to the number of lines. The function of these repetitions has been admirably stated by H. Womble in his study of this device in Horace:

iteration is neither accident of transmission nor carelessness on the part of the poet, but calculated design . . . its function is one of insistent recall. As such, repetition is an integral component of the poem's structure. Through recall it commands a backward glance, and in the inevitable re-evaluation of the preceding occurrence as well as in the enlarged reference of the subsequent, it furnishes a basis for parallel and emphasis (if the subsequent reinforces the preceding), or irony (if there results a re-interpretation or inversion). Recognition of the role played by this poetic device is therefore important for the full interpretation and for reaching the organic meaning of the poem.[38]

Womble refers to the role of repetition in revealing the structure of a poem; he might also have added that this device emphasizes the poem's predominant pattern of imagery. In Persius' Satires iteration serves both these purposes.

In this chapter I have suggested a different approach to a very difficult and complex poet. The traditional view of Persius, by overemphasizing the influence of his life upon his poetry, neglects his artistic achievement. Instead I propose to examine certain aspects of this achievement, to discover the underlying structure of individual Satires, and, hopefully, to define thereby the peculiar qualities of Persius' technique. This approach is deliberately limited and in no way discredits the valuable work already done on

---

oughly analyzes this technique. In the fifth Satire, for example, Cornutus says of Persius, *tu neque anhelanti, coquitur dum massa camino, / folle premis ventos* . . . (You do not compress your breath in gasping bellows while the mass of poetic ore bubbles on the forge, 10–11). This image is borrowed from Horace, *Ser.,* I.4.19–21:

> at tu conclusas hircinis follibus auras
> usque laborantis, dum ferrum molliat ignis,
> ut mavis, imitare.

Go ahead, if you prefer, and imitate the breath shut up in goatskin bellows, working continuously until the fire melts the iron.

As Kugler points out, p. 11, the verb *imitare* emphasizes the simile in these lines, but Persius has made the comparison more literal by describing the poet's mouth as a bellows (*folle*). Unfortunately Kugler does not discuss the relationship among the metaphors of an entire Satire.

[38] Hilburn Womble, "Repetition and Irony: Horace, *Odes* 2.18," *Trans. Amer. Philol. Assoc.* 92 (1961): p. 537.

such problems as the language of the Satires, Persius' debt to Stoicism, and his relationship to other writers. By discussing each work as a whole, however, I hope to show that Persius' Satires are unified poems rather than informal philosophic diatribes.

CHAPTER TWO

PROLOGUE

Nec fonte labra prolui caballino
nec in bicipiti somniasse Parnaso
memini, ut repente sic poeta prodirem.
Heliconidasque pallidamque Pirenen
illis remitto quorum imagines lambunt   5
hederae sequaces; ipse semipaganus
ad sacra vatum carmen adfero nostrum.
quis expedivit psittaco suum "chaere"
picamque docuit verba nostra conari?
magister artis ingenique largitor   10
venter, negatas artifex sequi voces.
quod si dolosi spes refulserit nummi,
corvos poetas et poetridas picas
cantare credas Pegaseium nectar.

I have not sloshed my lips in the nag's spring, nor do I remember having
dreamt on twin-peaked Parnassus and thus suddenly shot up a poet.
I leave the maids of Helicon and pale Pirene to those whose busts the
obsequious ivy licks; I, in spirit part peasant, through my own efforts
offer my poetry at the shrines of the bards. Who coaxed the greeting
"chaere" from the parrot and taught the magpie to try our human
speech? The skillful teacher and briber of talent, the belly, a master at
imitating voices denied by nature. For whenever they spy the glimmer
of coins (playing tricks with talent), these crow poets and magpie
poetesses could make you believe they were spouting the nectar of
Pegasus.

These fourteen choliambics accompanying Persius' six Satires present several problems. It is not known whether they originally
formed a preface or an epilogue to the Satires; in one branch of the
manuscript tradition represented by P they are omitted and added
as a prologue by a second hand one hundred years after the first,
while in the other branch represented by A and B they appear as an

epilogue between the last Satire and the subscript of A.D. 402.[1] In addition, the apparent lack of logical connection between the first seven and last seven lines has led many scholars to conclude that this poem is composed of two unrelated fragments. Casaubon first pointed out the dichotomous nature of the poem, without, however, rejecting it as a single work.[2] Jahn attempted to answer his criticism by equating the poets in the beginning of the poem with the crow poets and magpie poetesses in the latter half. These lines, he argued, contrasted the feigned source of poetic inspiration, Apollo and the Muses, with the real source, hunger, and they were primarily related to the first Satire rather than to all the Satires.[3] Fifty years later F. Leo rejected Jahn's view, suggesting instead that these lines represented two separate epigrams which Persius' friends, Cornutus and Bassus, found in his papers after his death and added as a preface to the posthumous edition of the Satires. Leo also conjectured that two Horatian passages inspired these epigrams, the first, *Ser.*, I.4.39–40, *primum ego me illorum dederim quibus esse poetas / excerpam numero* (first, I will exclude myself from the number of those I concede are poets), and the second, *Epis.*, II.2.51–52, *paupertas impulit audax / ut versus facerem* (reckless poverty forced me to try my hand at verse).[4] Later editors of the Satires, including those who consider the prologue a unified poem, often cite these passages, although, as Gaar first pointed out, Persius would hardly identify himself with the crow poets whom he is attacking.[5]

While a few critics still agree with Leo, most scholars now accept

[1] Wendell V. Clausen, "Sabinus' MS of Persius," *Hermes* 91 (1963): pp. 254–255, argues very plausibly that in the copy of Persius which Sabinus corrected in A.D. 402 the choliambics preceded the Satires and together with the subscript, which appeared between the choliambics and the first Satire, formed the first page. Sometime before A.D. 527, when the exemplar α was made, this first page came loose and was added on to the end of the book. In this way the choliambics became an epilogue placed between the sixth Satire and the subscript. Clausen also believes (p. 254, n. 3) that the first page of the exemplar of P came loose but was lost instead of being added on to the end of the book.

[2] Isaac Casaubon, ed., *Auli Persi Flacci Saturarum Liber* (Paris, 1605): Commentary, p. 3.

[3] Otto Jahn, ed., *Auli Persii Flacci Satirarum Liber, cum scholiis antiquis* (Leipzig, 1843), p. 71.

[4] F. Leo, "Zum Text des Persius und Iuvenal," *Hermes* 45 (1910): p. 48. The scholiast on line 10 of the prologue first suggested that hunger prompted Persius to write. Alfred Pretor, "A Few Notes on the *Satires* of Persius with Special Reference to the Purport and Position of the Prologue," *Class. Rev.* 21 (1907): pp. 72–74, argues that Persius adopted this pose in order to criticize Nero with impunity.

[5] E. Gaar, "Persiusprobleme," *Wien. Stud.* 31–32 (1909–1910): p. 131.

Jahn's view that the prologue is a single poem.[6] Very few, however, have attempted a poetic reading of these lines; instead they prefer to discuss when Persius composed the prologue, whether he modeled it on a similar poem by Lucilius, and whether he was influenced by the prologue to the *Aitia* or by the *Iambi* of Callimachus.[7] Admittedly these are important problems but they cannot be adequately discussed until the meaning of the poem is established. Specifically, what connection exists between the poets in the first half of the poem and those in the second half? Where does Persius stand in relation to both these groups of poets? What is the meaning of *semipaganus*? And why does Persius emphasize mimicry and imitation? In a recent article E. C. Witke suggests that the prologue establishes Persius' persona and as such "should no longer be considered a serious vehicle of information, but a cynical (or pseudo-cynical) statement of artistic intent and self-revelation."[8] Witke's approach is promising but his interpretation is only partially successful. He considers Persius' claim to be a *vates* a conventional one and argues that most of his remarks are rhetorically motivated.[9] Although I agree that in this prologue Persius develops one (but not his only) persona, I believe

[6] Among the critics who accept Leo's thesis are Paul Thomas, "Notes critiques et explicatives sur les "Satires" de Perse," *Bull. de l'acad. roy. de Belg.* Cl. des lett. (1920): pp. 45–66; André Cartault, "Les Choliambes de Perse," *Rev. de philol.* 45 (1921): pp. 63–65; and Enzo Marmorale, *Persio* (2nd ed., Florence, 1956), pp. 330–344. Hereafter I have referred to the choliambics as a prologue because I believe that, regardless of when they were written or how they were published, they express Persius' conception of his satire and are therefore prefatory in nature.

[7] On the date of the choliambics, see Gaar (1909–1910a), pp. 234–240 (A.D. 59); G. Gerhard, "Der Prolog des Persius," *Philologus* 72 (1913): pp. 484–491 (an early work); and G. Rambelli, "I coliambi di Persio," *Studi di filologia classica* (Pavia, 1957): pp. 3–8 (after some of the Satires). In regard to Persius' dependence upon Lucilius, the passage in the *Vita* which refers to this is usually interpreted to mean that Persius based his first Satire upon the tenth book of Lucilius. E. Gaar, "Persius und Lucilius," *Wien. Stud.* 31–32 (1909–1910): pp. 244–249, argues that the author of the *Vita* refers to the choliambics rather than to the first Satire. R. Reitzenstein, "Zur römischen Satire: zu Persius und Lucilius," *Hermes* 59 (1924): pp. 1–22, suggests that Persius modeled his preface on a similar choliambic preface to the tenth book of Lucilius, and he cites the verse quoted in *Satyricon*, 5 in support of his argument. Finally, the problem of Persius' debt to Callimachus is discusssed by Mario Puelma Piwonka, *Lucilius und Kallimachos* (Frankfurt, 1949), pp. 359–367, and W. Wimmel, *Kallimachos in Rom*, Hermes Einzelschriften, 16 (Wiesbaden, 1960), pp. 309–311. Cf. also Christopher Dawson's remarks on Callimachus' influence upon the Roman satirists in general in "The Iambi of Callimachus," *Yale Class. Stud.* 11 (1950): pp. 138–140.

[8] E. C. Witke (1962), p. 158.

[9] *Ibid.*, p. 154.

that behind the pose of the angry young poet Persius is seriously stating his artistic creed.

In the first Satire Persius attacks his fellow poets' taste for mythological and pastoral poetry written in slavish imitation of the Greeks. Here in the prologue he repeats this charge and suggests the more worthwhile alternative of upholding Roman values in a native literary genre, satire. Thus in the opening lines he rejects Hippocrene, Helicon, Parnassus, and Pirene not simply because they are traditional sources of inspiration but, much more importantly, because they are Greek sources. At the same time he affirms his lack of dependence upon the famous poets associated with these geographic symbols, Hesiod, Callimachus, and Ennius.[10] Ennius is included because although he was the national poet of early Rome he drew his inspiration from Homer and in the opening of the *Annales* he invoked the Olympian Muses instead of the native Roman *Camenae*. Persius emphasizes his disrespect for the Greek tradition by referring contemptuously to Hippocrene as *fonte caballino* and, as Witke notes, by suggesting that one could forget a vision such as Ennius'.[11] In visualizing Ennius asleep on the bumpy twin peaks of this mountain, skillfully emphasized in the tribrach *bicipiti*, Persius further ridicules the epic poet.[12] Lines 4 and 5 hint at the emptiness of this approach to poetry; Pirene is characterized as *pallidam*, lifeless and uninspiring, while the *imagines* of the poets displayed after their death are equally inanimate. These opening lines thus satirize both the famous names in Greek literature and the early Roman writers who imitated them; in addition Persius implicitly attacks his contemporaries, particularly those in Nero's literary circle, who slav-

---

[10] Cf. Hesiod, *Theog.*, 1 ff., *Anth. Palat.*, VII.42 (*re* Callimachus), Lucretius, I.117, and Propertius, III.3.1 (*re* Ennius). Ennius himself acknowledged his philhellenism (Aulus Gellius, XVII.17.1), and both Suetonius, *De gramm.*, I.2 and *Festus*, 412.33 regard him as part Greek. It is easier, I think, to explain Ennius' presence here in this way than to maintain, as Witke (1962), p. 154, does, that Ennius represents a Latin tradition. Giovanni d'Anna, "Persio *semipaganus*," *Riv. di cult. class. e medioev.* 6 (1964): pp. 181–185, notes two significant echoes in lines 5–6 of Propertius, II.5.26 and IV.1.61–64. Cf. also J. Waszink, "The Proem of the Annales of Ennius," *Mnemosyne* 4, 3 (1950): pp. 214–240 and "Retractio Enniana," *Mnemosyne* 4, 15 (1962): pp. 113–132.

[11] Witke (1962), p. 154. I would also agree with Gaar (1909–1910a), p. 131, that the allusions to Pegasus in the opening and closing lines are an additional argument for considering the prologue a unified poem.

[12] Waszink (1962), p. 127. Waszink also believes, p. 128, that Ennius' vision of Homer occurred on Helicon but that Persius deliberately misplaced it on Parnassus to deride him.

ishly copied Greek models and specialized in mythological and pastoral themes. By stressing the derivative character of contemporary poetry Persius introduces the theme of imitation which he develops in the latter half of the poem.

In lines 6 and 7, the central lines of the poem, Persius presents his concept of his own poetry.[13] He calls himself *semipaganus,* a word coined for the occasion, meaning "half-rustic," and represents himself bringing his poems as an offering to the shrine of the *vates.* The significance of this persona offers a clue to the identity of these *vates.* Throughout Latin poetry the Roman farmer appears as the representative of pure Roman culture untainted by foreign influences and the upholder of old Roman virtues.[14] The act of dedicating the first fruits of labor at a country shrine is equally evocative of the old Roman religion. Understood in this context *vates* can only refer to native Roman writers of the past. Appropriately, the term *vates* is not Greek, unlike the epithet of the Greek writers and their imitators, *poetae.* The strong religious connotation of *vates* renders it even more suitable in this context. In saying that he dedicates his *carmen* to these native writers Persius emphasizes his role as representative of the Roman poetic tradition. The adjective *nostrum* means "mine" versus "theirs," but, more important, "ours" as Romans versus "theirs" as Greeks.[15] Together these two lines express Persius' concept of his satire. While he will not hesitate to use a colloquial vocabulary and style, he will also draw freely upon the devices of more elevated poetry (*carmen*), such as *allegoria,* personification, and complex imagery. Above all, his satire will oppose the Hellenizing trend of his time and urge men to rediscover the old Roman virtues. Reading these lines one cannot help noticing how carefully Persius has established an image of himself as a peculiarly Roman poet writing in the only genre invented by the Romans, satire.

In the last seven lines of the prologue Persius explicitly disassociates himself from the poets of his own day who, he says, are bribed to ape Nero's philhellenism and imitate his poetic efforts. The controlling metaphor in these lines is that of the client-patron relationship, specifically the emperor as a literary patron to his clients,

[13] This is one of Persius' favorite devices, cf. *infra,* n. 47.

[14] Cf. Persius, VI.37–39, Juvenal, III.67–68.

[15] Gaar (1909–1910a), p. 129, n. 6, points out that H. Küster, *De A. Persii Flacci elocutione quaestiones* (Löbau, 1894–1897, n.v.) 2: p. 13, remarked upon the similarity between this *nostrum* and Quintilian, X.1.93, *Satira quidem tota nostra est.* Cf. also Cicero's use of *noster, infra, p.* 32.

the court poets.[16] The parrot is a particularly suitable symbol of servility to the emperor because by tradition the parrot was often given to rulers as an exotic present and although he had to be taught most phrases, he knew by nature how to salute his master and say *ave, Caesar*.[17] Pliny and Statius both refer to this tradition, and to Martial the parrot perhaps symbolizes the expediency of flattering the emperor: *Psittacus a vobis aliorum nomina discam, / hoc didici per me dicere: CAESAR HAVE* (I, the parrot, will learn others' names from you; this I have taught myself to say: "Hail Caesar," XIV.73).[18] Furthermore, Macrobius relates that after the battle of Actium several trained crows and a magpie greeted Octavian as victor. The latter bought them all and a shoemaker, perceiving the profit in this trick, taught a crow to salute Octavian. The future emperor refused this bird with the wry comment, *satis domi salutatorum talium habeo* (I have enough well-wishers of this kind at home).[19] This anecdote suggests that the comparison between a talking bird and the client would not seem far-fetched to a Roman. Persius' reference to the parrot clearly incorporates this tradition but instead of the usual salutation, *ave, Caesar*, Persius' parrot says *chaere*. Through this minor alteration Persius evokes two further associations. First, in a well-known fragment of Lucilius, Scaevola attacks a contemporary, Albucius, for his affected Greek ways:

Graecum te, Albuci, quam Romanum atque Sabinum,
municipem Ponti, Tritani, centurionum,
praeclarorum hominum ac primorum, signiferumque
maluisti dici. Graece ergo praetor Athenis,
id quod maluisti, te, cum ad me accedis,
    saluto:
chaere, inquam, Tite. lictores, turma omnis
chorusque ⟨cohorsque⟩:

[16] Although Casaubon and several other scholars have seen the prologue as an attack upon Nero and his literary circle, they have not, to my knowledge, based their view upon a close literary analysis of the imagery in the poem.

[17] Cf. the scholion on line 8, describing the parrot:

ex natura salutans *ave* vel *chere*, quae pro munere offertur regibus. Nam cetera verba institutione (i.e. doctrina) discit.

Of its own accord it offers greetings, saying "hail" in Latin or Greek, and for this reason it is often presented as a gift to kings. It can also be taught other words.

[18] Pliny, *Hist. Nat.*, X.58.117, Statius, *Silvae*, II.4.29–30. Cf. Otto Weinreich, *Studien zu Martial* (Stuttgart, 1928), pp. 113–114.

[19] Macrobius, *Sat.*, II.4.29–30. As Reitzenstein notes, p. 3, Persius' reference to *poetridas picas* more probably alludes to the legend of the nine daughters of Pierus and Euippe who challenged the Muses to a poetry contest and for their arrogance were turned into magpies (Ovid, *Met.*, V.250 ff.).

"chaere, Tite." Hinc hostis mi Albucius,
  hinc inimicus [88–94].

You, Albucius, would rather be called a Greek than a Roman and
Sabine, a fellow-countryman of Pontius and Tritanus, from a family of
centurions, outstanding men, and standard bearers. Therefore I, a
praetor, greet you at Athens in Greek, as you prefer, when we meet;
"chaere, Titus," I say. My lictors and all my attendants echo in chorus,
"chaere, Titus." For this reason, Albucius is my enemy and unfriendly
to me.

Several scholars have noted the relevance of this passage but they
generally overlook the context in which these lines are preserved in
Cicero's *De finibus*, I.9.[20] Cicero rebukes the Latin writers for ignoring their own literary tradition in favor of Greek models. Before
quoting Lucilius he comments:

Quis enim tam inimicus paene nomini Romano est, qui Ennii Medeam
aut Antiopam Pacuvii spernat aut reiciat, quod se isdem Euripidis
fabulis delectari dicat, Latinas litteras oderit? . . . A quibus tantum
dissentio ut, cum Sophocles vel optime scripserit Electram, tamen male
conversam Atilii mihi legendam putem. . . . Rudem enim esse omnino
in nostris poetis aut inertissimae segnitiae aut fastidii delicatissimi. Mihi
quidem nulli satis eruditi videntur, quibus nostra ignota sunt [I.4–5].

For who is so hostile to everything Roman that he scorns and rejects
Ennius' *Medea* and the *Antiope* of Pacuvius, and says that he delights
in the plays of Euripides but hates Latin literature? . . . I disagree with
these views so strongly that although Sophocles wrote an excellent
Electra, nevertheless I prefer to read the inferior version of Atilius. . . .
To remain completely ignorant of the works of our own poets is a
sign of either utter laziness or the most effete fastidiousness. Indeed,
no one, in my opinion, can claim to be cultivated who does not know our
own writers.

By changing *ave* to *chaere* Persius, I believe, intends the reader to
recall the earlier passage in Lucilius, and since his reasons for quoting the latter coincide with Cicero's he may also be alluding to this
passage in the *De finibus*. At any rate the substitution of *chaere* for
ave clearly underscores Persius' contempt for the philhellenism of
his time.

The metaphor of servile flattery toward the emperor suggested by
the reference to the parrot is made more explicit by the term *largitor*
(10). The common translation of this word, "bestower," is misleading; it has here the much more sinister connotation of "briber."

---

[20] Cf. Reitzenstein, p. 3, Reckford, p. 502, n. 1. Since Persius seems to mock
Ennius in the prologue and again in Satire VI, he would probably not endorse
Cicero's praise for him, but he would agree that Roman writers ought to
respect their own tradition. Cf. *infra,* n. 35.

During the later first century B.C. *largitio* denoted a bribe for political favors and, in particular, the rewards given to the lower classes for their loyalty and attendance as *sectatores* during the elections.[21] In the early empire this term generally referred to the donatives given by the emperor to secure the allegiance of his troops or the household in general. Tacitus and Suetonius both use it in this sense several times, and Juvenal applies the term to a patron's gift to his clients (V.110).[22] *Sequi*, too, is a verb often used with the connotation of political allegiance.[23] Literally, of course, in the prologue *largitor* refers to the poet's hunger which compels him to write the kind of verse his patron wishes to hear. But by playing upon the political connotations of *largitor* and *sequi*, Persius, I suggest, implies that Nero bribes the contemporary poets with promises of imperial patronage and financial rewards to flatter him and mimic his poetic tastes. Thus in the final lines of the poem it is these contemporary poets (and poetesses) who are the *corvos poetas et poetridas picas* and who, having been bribed by Nero, write the kind of poetry he admires and are applauded so loudly by him that one might imagine they had written good verse.[24] The money which they receive is *dolosus* because it stimulates them to deceive the emperor by writing what he wishes to hear and because it encourages him to applaud bad poetry simply because he has paid for it. Finally, the conscious echoes of *poeta* (3, 13), *sequi* (11) and *sequaces* (6), *caballino* (1) and *Pegaseium* (14) relate these contemporary imitators to their earlier counterparts.

While this reading does not claim to be definitive, it does unite the two halves of the poem by the theme of obsequious servility to another's literary standards. In the first seven lines Persius rejects the standards set by poets outside his own native tradition; in the last seven he equally scorns those established by the corrupted writers of his day. The themes of independence versus servility and imitation, Roman versus Greek, and *rusticitas* versus *urbanitas* intertwine throughout the poem, giving it structural unity. And although one need not consider this prologue solely as an attack upon Nero,

[21] Cf. Cicero, *Cat.*, IV.5 (*largitor*), *Planc.*, XV.37 (*largitor*), *Mur.*, XXXVI.77, *Leg.*, III.17.39; Sallust, *Cat.*, III.3, *Jug.*, CIII.6; Nepos, *Milt.*, VI.4.

[22] Tacitus, *Ann.*, I.52, II.55, XII.69, *Hist.*, II.82, 94; Suetonius, *Aug.*, X.3, *Tib.*, XLVIII.2, *Claud.*, XXIX.1, *Nero*, XXX.2 *Vit.* XV.1. Cf. Velleius, II.20.4, Juvenal, VII.88.

[23] Cicero, *Amic.*, XII.41; Tacitus, *Ann.*, II.43, XII.69, *Hist.*, II.86, IV.37.

[24] If the phrase *poetridas picas* is taken literally to refer to poetesses, Persius must be satirizing the bluestockings of his day.

the emphasis upon the Hellenizing tastes of the time, as well as
the connotations of the parrot image and the term *largitor,* support
such an interpretation.[25]

SATIRE I

Buffon's well-known observation, "Style is the man," conveniently
summarizes the theme of the first Satire. Buffon was not the first to
define style in this manner, however, for the idea appears much
earlier in the Greek proverb οἷος ὁ βίος, τοιοῦτος καὶ ὁ λόγος (As a
man's way of life is, so also is his speech).[26] This proverb reflects the
classical view of external characteristics as trustworthy indications
of character, among which speech was particularly important because of the oral emphasis in classical literature. As a proverb this
saying cannot be dated, but it appears to be echoed in a remark
of Socrates in the *Republic.* After arguing that good and bad
rhythm, as well as harmony and disharmony, depend upon style,
Socrates asks:

Τί δ'ὁ τρόπος τῆς λέξεως, ἦν δ'ἐγώ, καὶ ὁ λόγος; οὐ τῷ τῆς ψυχῆς ἤθει
ἕπεται;
Πῶς γὰρ οὔ;
Τῇ δὲ λέξει τἄλλα;
Ναί [400d].

What about the style of speaking, I said, and speech itself? Does it not
follow the moral character of the soul?
Certainly.
And all else follows the style of speaking?
Yes.

This idea appealed particularly to the Stoics with their interest in
literature as well as moral philosophy. During a discussion of the
good life in the *Tusculan Disputations* Cicero recalls Socrates'
words:

Nos autem volumus [vitam] beatissimam, idque nobis Socratica illa
conclusione confirmatur. Sic enim princeps ille philosophiae disserebat:
qualis cuiusque animi adfectus esset, talem esse hominem, qualis autem

---

[25] It is possible to interpret these lines as referring, more generally, to the
aristocratic patrons and their clients. Cf. *infra,* p. 38.
[26] Cf. A. Otto, *Die Sprichwörter und sprichwörtlichen Redensarten der Römer*
(Leipzig, 1890), p. 257, and Niall Rudd, "The Style and the Man," *Phoenix* 18
(1964): pp. 216–231.

homo ipse esset, talem eius esse orationem; orationi autem facta similia, factis vitam [V.16.47].

We, however, wish the happiest life possible, and this is proved by that Socratic syllogism. For thus the leader of philosophy used to reason: as each man's soul is, so also is the man, and as a man is, so also is his speech. Furthermore his deeds reflect his speech, and his life reflects his deeds.

This concept of style accounts for the frequent appearance of physical or sexual metaphors in classical literary criticism.[27] In the mid-first century A.D., moreover, and particularly during Nero's reign, when Persius was writing, this metaphor becomes a commonplace. Nero's outrageous behavior accelerated the already rapid decay of morals while his philhellenism provoked a corresponding decline in literature. Although very little court poetry of this period has survived, the extant examples, such as the bucolic poetry of Calpurnius Siculus, the Einsiedeln eclogues, and the fragments attributed to Nero, illustrate the kind of verse derided by Persius. This poetry combines imitation of the obscure allusions, rich descriptions, and soft euphonious rhythms of the Alexandrian school with fulsome flattery of Nero.[28] It is not surprising, therefore, to find the critics of the period relating the rise of this enervated poetry to the increasing effeminacy in society. In *Epistle* CXIV, for example, Seneca treats this topic at length and quotes the Greek proverb, which he translates *talis hominibus fuit oratio qualis vita*. By choosing Maecenas as his major example Seneca adroitly avoids criticizing Nero and his court directly while at the same time he attacks the Maecenases of his day, the wealthy aristocrats, intimates of the emperor, and bad amateur poets. These are the same men whom Persius criticizes in his first Satire. The adjectives which Seneca applies to the contemporary literary style, such as *infracta, lasciva, soluta,* and *tenera,* are equally descriptive of the human body; in contrast he calls for a style which is *robusta, virilis,* and *fortis.*

Petronius offers further parallels to Persius' first Satire. The

[27] Cf. Larue Van Hook, *The Metaphorical Terminology of Greek Rhetoric and Literary Criticism* (Diss., University of Chicago, 1905), p. 26, and A. Desmouliez, "La Signification esthétique des comparaisons entre le style et le corps humain dans la rhétorique antique," *Rev. étud. lat.* 33 (1955): p. 59, which is unfortunately only a summary of a paper.

[28] A general survey of this literature will be found in F. Bücheler, "Zur höfischen Poesie unter Nero," *Rhein. Mus.* 26 (1871): pp. 235-240, reprinted in his *Kleine Schriften* (Leipzig/Berlin, 1927) 2: pp. 1-6; H. Bardon, "Les poésies de Néron," *Rev. étud. lat.* 14 (1936): pp. 337-349, and *Les Empereurs et les lettres latines d'Auguste à Hadrien* (Paris, 1940), pp. 191-256; and M. A. Levi, *Nerone e i suoi tempi* (Milan, 1949), pp. 76-81.

extant portion of the *Satyricon* opens in the middle of Encolpius'
tirade against rhetoric, in the course of which he refers to contemporary oratory as *mellitos verborum globulos et omnia dicta
factaque quasi papavere et sesamo sparsa* (honey balls of words, and
all speeches and deeds sprinkled, as it were, with poppy and sesame
seeds, 1), an image which recalls the frequent references to poetry
as food in Persius' first and fifth Satires.[29] Encolpius also complains
that

ac ne carmen quidem sani coloris enituit, sed omnia quasi eodem cibo
pasta non potuerunt usque ad senectutem canescere [2].

not even poetry shines with a healthy complexion; every kind of literary
expression, fed on the same pap, fails to reach white-haired old age.

This comparison echoes Persius' allusions to pale poets old before
their time (11, 26). Agamemnon's defense of the rhetoricians is
equally reminiscent of Persius. He compares them to *ficti adulatores*
who are forced to flatter in order to eat, and he adds that they will
lose students

nisi quasdam insidias auribus fecerint: sic eloquentiae magister, nisi
tanquam piscator eam imposuerit hamis escam, quam scierit appetituros
esse pisciculos, sine spe praedae morabitur in scopulo [3].

unless they "ambush" their ears; for if the teacher of eloquence does not
bait his hook, like the fisherman, with some tidbit he knows the little fish
will snap at, he will waste his time on the rock without hope of a catch.

The word *escam* (food, tidbit) appears in a similar context in the
first Satire (22), and the phrase *insidias auribus* (ambushes of the
ears) reminds one of Persius' frequent allusions to ears (22, 59, 108,
126).

Two other writers deserve mention here, for although they wrote
after Persius they describe the same decay of literature and morals
in similar terms. Quintilian, in an elaborate simile, compares the
eloquence of his day to a castrated slave boy, and then concludes:

Quapropter eloquentiam, licet hanc (ut sentio enim, dicam), libidinosam
resupina voluptate auditoria probent, nullam esse existimabo, quae ne
minimum quidem in se indicium masculi et incorrupti, ne dicam gravis
et sancti viri, ostentet [V.12.20].[30]

Although audiences may admire the effeminate charms of this sensual
(for I speak my own feelings) eloquence, I will not consider it eloquence
at all; for it does not give the slightest proof that its author is virile and
uncorrupted, let alone a just man worthy of respect.

[29] Cf. *infra*, pp. 34, 72, 76.

[30] George Kennedy, "An Estimate of Quintilian," *Amer. Jour. of Philol.*
83 (1962): p. 137, n. 24, suggests that Domitian's prohibition of castration (cf.
Suetonius, *Domit.*, VII) inspired this unusual simile.

The allusions to homosexuality here are particularly relevant to the poetry recitation which Persius describes (15–21). In Tacitus' *Dialogus de oratoribus,* which reflects conditions in A.D. 75, Messalla asks:

Quis enim ignorat et eloquentiam et ceteras artes descivisse ab ista vetere gloria, non inopia hominum sed desidia iuventutis et negligentia parentum et inscientia praecipientium et oblivione moris antiqui? [XXVIII]

Who is not aware that eloquence and the other arts have lost their former renown, due not to a shortage of practitioners but to the laziness of the younger generation, the negligence of their parents, the ignorance of their teachers, and the failure to remember earlier customs?

It is also interesting that it is the defender of contemporary rhetoric in this dialogue, Aper, who says:

Exigitur enim iam ab oratore etiam poeticus decor, non Accii aut Pacuvii veterno inquinatus, sed ex Horatii et Vergilii et Lucani sacrario prolatus. . . . Neque ideo minus efficaces sunt orationes nostrae, quia ad aures iudicantium cum voluptate perveniunt [XX].[31]

Now even the orator must cultivate a poetic style, not one tainted by the archaism of Accius and Pacuvius, but one drawn from the shrine of Horace, Vergil and Lucan. . . . And our speeches are no less effective because they charm the jurors' ears.

Aper shares the distaste of Persius' adversary for Pacuvius and Accius (76–77), and resembles Pedius in his attitude toward court oratory (85–87).

If the theme of Persius' first Satire is conventional, however, his treatment of it is not. Although the poem appears to be a satiric apologia, comparison with Seneca's epistle suggests that Persius is more interested in exploring the moral problem of how the decay in contemporary literature reflects a physical and spiritual decay in society.[32] Because he is not writing a program Satire, strictly speaking, he reacts flippantly toward the warnings of his adversary and devotes only a small portion of the poem to his own defense. Behind a carefully controlled façade of spontaneous conversation the

---

[31] For the date see Ronald Syme, *Tacitus* (Oxford, 1958) 2: p. 670.

[32] Lucius Shero, "The Satirist's Apologia," *Univ. Wis. Stud. in Lang. and Lit.* 15 (1922), pp. 148–167, points out the stock apologetic elements in this Satire and in Horace, *Ser.,* II.1 and Juvenal, I.1. In arguing for a moral purpose behind Persius' literary criticism, I disagree with André Cartault, "La Satire I de Perse," *Rev. de philol.* 45 (1921): p. 69, who says of the poetry which Persius attacks: "Its impression upon the listeners is one of purely physical pleasure. It is not at all a question of licentious poetry, but simply of the sensual effect of the verbal harmony, and the critics are wrong in seeing allusions in this Satire to the corruption of morals; it is only a question of the corruption of taste."

Satire falls into three major sections. In the first Persius rejects the contemporary literary audience (1–12), in the second he attacks three aspects of contemporary poetry (13–106), and in the third he defends satire and describes the kind of audience he wants (107–134). The first and third sections clearly complement each other, the first twelve lines rejecting the contemporary audience being balanced by the last twelve describing the ideal reader.

The second section, by far the longest, is subdivided into three parts, each treating one aspect of contemporary poetry. To illustrate his thesis that this poetry emphasizes external effects, Persius first criticizes it from this viewpoint (13–62). He alludes in passing to the subject matter of this verse (34, 50), but concentrates his attention upon the poets' clothes (15–16, 32), the titillating effect of their delivery (19–21, 36), and their desire for appreciation and praise (28, 36–43). Externals are emphasized in the adversary's need to show his learning (24–25), and in the image of praise worn as a garment (49–50). These lines also include two contrasted poetry recitations, one in public (*populo*, 15–21), and one at a private dinner (30–40). The deliberate similarity between these scenes suggests that the current decay in taste affects all classes.

In the second subsection Persius attacks the content of contemporary poetry (62–91). The lines, *ecce modo heroas sensus adferre docemus / nugari solitos Graece* (look, now we teach poets used to dabbling in Greek to produce heroic emotions, 69–70), refer to the two genres popular in the first century A.D., epic and pastoral. Persius urges that the Roman countryside replace the Greek in pastoral and that the epic poets treat historical events from their own tradition. In the last lines of this section (83–91), Persius states a theme implicit in his earlier criticism, that is, that poetry must deal with truth. Pedius represents the perversion of truth in its most important domain, the law courts.

The third subsection, like the second, is introduced by the adversary (92–106). In this section Persius attacks the techniques of contemporary poetry, illustrating his remarks with several anonymous verses (99–102). These verses contain conspicuous faults of the period: the absence of elision, monotonous word order, lack of rhythmic variety, and an excessive Greek vocabulary.[33] The subject matter, a frenzied Bacchic orgy, and the references to the Maenads

---

[33] Villeneuve (1918a), pp. 208–218, analyzes these verses thoroughly and concludes, p. 224, that they are not by Nero. Bardon (1940), pp. 204–205, attributes them to Nero and even admires them.

and Attis support Persius' previous contention that contemporary poets are only interested in mythological subjects fraught with emotion (34, 69–70).

Much of the vitality of this Satire derives from the care with which Persius develops his own persona, the young poet already introduced in the prologue, and that of his adversary, the contemporary poetaster. In contrast to the latter, whom he derides as old (22), impotent (23), bald (56), and obese (57), and to the "censorious uncles" (patruos, 11) of his time, Persius plays the puer (113), the young, virile poet, full of energy and scorn.[34] He is not the familiar angry young poet, however, for instead of rejecting his own literary tradition he values it. Ignorance of this tradition, he argues, epitomized by his adversary's scorn for Pacuvius and Accius, accounts for the present decline in literature.[35] He urges the poets to turn to their own history, to the stories of Remus and Cincinnatus, for inspiration and he reminds the aristocrats of their heritage by the epithets which he applies to them, Titos (20), Romulidae (31), and Romule (87).

Intellectual arrogance often characterizes the laudator temporis

[34] By comparing himself to a puer Persius evokes the truth and honesty associated with a juvenile viewpoint.

[35] Lines 76–78 have provoked much debate about whether Persius or the adversary is here ridiculing Accius and Pacuvius. Most editors attribute these lines to Persius, arguing that he could not have admired the roughness of early Latin poetry and therefore must be indirectly attacking the archaizers of his time. But since it is the adversary, himself an effeminate poet, who appreciates the soft, enervated rhythms of contemporary verse, it is more likely that he criticizes the roughness of earlier writers while Persius admires the robust, virile quality of their poetry. Admittedly in the prologue Persius criticizes the early Roman writers for their philhellenism, but there he attacks not their rough style so much as their preference for Greek rather than Roman subject matter. Here in the first Satire there is a shift of emphasis to the decline in literary style and a corresponding shift in attitude toward these earlier writers. This is a good example of how the satirist varies his views according to the requirements of his theme and his persona. I would therefore attribute lines 76–78 to the adversary; in reply Persius says to his reader, "When you see blind fathers pour warnings such as these into their sons, do you wonder where that verbal hash comes from?" (79–81). He deliberately refers to the adversary's words by the demonstrative hos to clarify his meaning. I have translated lippos as "blind" rather than "bleary-eyed" to capture its metaphorical meaning of "intellectually deceived." In support of this interpretation, see H. J. Rose, "Some Traps in Persius' First Satire," Class. Rev. 38 (1924): pp. 63–64, and R. Marache, La Critique littéraire de langue latine et le développement du goût archaïsant au IIe siècle de notre ère (Rennes, 1952), pp. 34–35. Marache points out that Persius is the only first-century author to admire such early writers as Pacuvius and Accius; most people considered Vergil and Horace early enough. The adversary in the first Satire, attempting to be very modern, even scorns Vergil (96–97).

acti and Persius' persona is no exception. He insists that his readers be familiar with Old Comedy, tolerant of criticism, and willing to accept didactic satire (*aliquid decoctius*, 125).[36] The two types which he rejects as readers contrast sharply with this ideal audience. The first, a semi-educated man, sneers at Greek sandals instead of studying Greek literature and, ignorant of his own soul, laughs at the physical defects of others. He also assumes that his ability to correct market measures qualifies him to evaluate literature; here Persius derides both the common reader's habit of acting as literary censor and his assumption that there is only one standard of measurement. The second man, completely uneducated and hostile to learning, whiles away his time in the Forum laughing at itinerant mathematicians and philosophers.

The facetious wit of Persius' persona succeeds in tempering his arrogance. He cheerfully acknowledges his lack of interest in popular praise and later, with mock resignation, agrees to all his adversary says. His most serious charge, that everyone has the ears of an ass, is treated as a witty secret which must be buried:

> me muttire nefas? nec clam? nec cum
>   scrobe? nusquam?
> hic tamen infodiam. vidi, vidi ipse,
>   libelle:
> auriculas asini quis non habet? [119–121]

Am I forbidden to whisper? Not even in secret? Nor in a hole? Not anywhere? Nevertheless I will bury it here. I have seen, I myself have seen, little book: who does not have the ears of an ass?

Furthermore he frequently includes himself in his criticism (11, 13, 69, 104), or adopts a tone of humble sincerity to win over his audience (45–47). Through these devices Persius creates an appealing persona appropriate to his purpose.

The adversary participates more fully in this poem than in any other. Hendrickson's theory that "Persius nowhere in the first satire employs dialogue," but instead creates an interior monologue is difficult to accept because the adversary is a conventional satiric device and in this Satire consistently drawn.[37] He reveals his identity gradually. His reaction to Persius' unpopularity, *turpe et miserabile*

---

[36] Witke (1961), p. 62, notes that this phrase also refers to Persius' compressed style. He paraphrases line 125: "If perchance you'd taste something less crude still, and more refined than your ordinary glass, something expanded in worth through contraction in bulk, read my satires as well." Cf. my earlier remarks on *allegoria, supra*, pp. 11–12.

[37] George Hendrickson, "The First Satire of Persius," *Class. Phil.* 23 (1928): pp. 102–107.

(shameful and deplorable, 3), implying in turn that he is eager for praise, suggests that he is a writer of some kind.[38] The fact that Persius admonishes him to ignore public opinion indicates that he is perhaps capable of independent judgment. But at this point, in order to draw our attention away from the adversary, Persius shifts to the first person plural and begins to describe an unknown poet; then, by the unobtrusive verb *leges* (you will read, 17), he suddenly identifies the adversary with this poet, an impotent homosexual who craves recognition of his obscure erudition.

The adversary's next remark, *at pulchrum est digito monstrari et dicier "hic est"* (but it is grand to be pointed out with the words, "This is he," 28), alludes to a well-known anecdote about Demosthenes told by Cicero, Pliny the Younger, and Aelian.[39] In the *Tusculan Disputations* Cicero chides Demosthenes for his love of praise:

> Num igitur ignobilitas aut humilitas
> aut etiam popularis offensio sapientem
> beatum esse prohibebit? Vide ne plus
> commendatio in vulgus et haec quae ex-
> petitur gloria molestiae habet quam
> voluptatis. Leviculus sane noster
> Demosthenes, qui illo susurro delectari
> se dicebat aquam ferentis mulierculae,
> ut mos in Graecia est, insusurrantisque
> alteri, "Hic est ille Demosthenes."
> Quid hoc levius? at quantus orator!
> Sed apud alios loqui videlicet didicerat,
> non multum ipse secum [V.36.103].

Will low birth, therefore, or humility, or even the public's hostility prevent a wise man from being happy? Remember that popularity and renown, actively sought, often bring more discomfort than pleasure. Our Demosthenes showed his frivolous side when he admitted that he was delighted by the whispers of the women carrying home water, as is the custom in Greece, and murmuring to one another, "This is the famous Demosthenes." What could be more frivolous than this? And

---

[38] The distribution of dialogue in Clausen's edition (1956) has been adopted in this discussion. Almost every critic who has written on the first Satire arranges the opening dialogue differently; the latest suggestion is that of M. L. West, "Persius i. 1–3," *Class. Rev.* 11 (1961): p. 204. The ambiguity of the phrase *turpe et miserabile* should not be overlooked; in one sense it signifies the adversary's concern with praise, but in another it expresses Persius' own opinion: it *is* shameful that the public ignores criticism instead of benefitting from it. Note, too, the moral overtones of *turpe, turbida, improbum,* and *castiges* which suggest that more than poetry is being criticized. Cf. *infra,* p. 33.

[39] Pliny, *Epis.,* IX.23, Aelian, *Vera Hist.,* IX.17. Cf. also Horace, *Odes,* IV.3.22.

yet what an orator he was! Obviously he had learned to talk to others, but seldom to himself.

Although Persius perhaps heard this anecdote from some other source, he may also have read it in Cicero. In any case the preceding exclamation, *o mores* (26), echoing Cicero's famous *o tempora, o mores* (*Cat.*, I.1), suggests that Persius intended his readers to recall the Ciceronian passage. The phrase *hic est* is borrowed directly from Cicero and the latter's judgment of Demosthenes, *apud alios loqui videlicet didicerat, non multum ipse secum,* recalls Persius' earlier warning to his adversary, *nec te quaesiveris extra* (do not seek self-knowledge from without, 7), which alludes to the Greek maxim, "Know thyself" (cf. p. 33). Furthermore, Cicero implies that such a desire for public recognition conflicts with the Stoic virtue of αὐτάρκεια (self-sufficiency). By recalling this passage in the *Tusculan Disputations,* therefore, Persius confirms his adversary's lack of self-knowledge and inability to follow Stoicism.

We now know that the adversary is a vain, effeminate poet deaf to philosophic reason. In line 40 through the unexpected appearance of *ait,* "he says," Persius acknowledges the existence of us, his audience. At the same time he prepares us for the sudden revelation in line 44 that the adversary is imaginary. By conceding this Persius shrewdly suggests that he is more sincere with his readers than those writers who maintain the fiction of dialogue; he thereby increases our confidence in him. He does not intend to have us disbelieve all that the adversary says, however, simply because he is fictitious, for he continues to address him throughout the Satire and to develop his character. Paradoxically, Persius is able to momentarily deny the reality of his adversary only because he has made him such a vivid character.

In lines 53–61 Persius further defines the adversary as an aristocratic literary patron who expects applause from his clients in return for dinner. He is bald, obese, and niggardly toward his client, giving him only a *trita lacerna* (worn cloak, 54). In the long passage which follows (63–106), an attack on the subjects and techniques of modern poetry, the adversary's interjections demonstrate his poor literary taste: he describes poetry as if it were comparable to drafting or perhaps pointing a statue (65–66), he scorns Accius, Pacuvius, and Vergil (76–78, 96–97), and he quotes the specimens or parodies of contemporary verse (99–102). In passing, Persius also suggests that the adversary uses his appearances in court as excuses to display his meager literary talent (83–84).

The adversary clearly misses the point of all this criticism, for after Persius has exposed the evils in literature and society he still asks:

> sed quid opus teneras mordaci radere vero
> auriculas? vide sis ne maiorum tibi forte
> limina frigescant: sonat hic de nare
> canina
> littera [107–110].

But why is it necessary to scrape tender ears with sharp truth? Take care that the thresholds of the rich do not freeze you out, for in this criticism of yours satire snarls through the nose.

Ironically, he calls the aristocrats' ears *auriculas,* a word which has already been used to describe the ears of an ass (59), and he further qualifies them as *teneras,* suggesting effeminacy.[40] The phrase *sonat hic de nare canina / littera* is generally taken, following the scholia, to refer to the reaction of those aristocrats who are criticized.[41] Anderson, however, suggests that *hic* means *in satura* because the canine letter, *r,* is found in the word *satura* and both Lucilius and Horace use canine imagery to describe satire.[42] His translation of this line, "here [in satire] there is the nasal sound of the canine letter," although an improvement over the scholiast's interpretation, does not follow logically from the adversary's preceding remark. I suggest instead that *hic* means "in this criticism of yours," and the *canina littera* stands for satire. Then the adversary warns Persius that his satire may lose him influential patrons. In his explosive reply Persius compares the adversary to a man who paints snakes over a sacred spot to warn children not to defile it. This vivid image suggests a complete reversal of values; the adversary's bad tastes and standards have acquired inviolability and he regards satire as a dirty, puerile thing. At this point, when his ignorance and prudishness have rendered him useless, Persius dismisses him.

The dominant metaphor in this Satire equates the poets literally and physically with the poems they write. They use their poetry as they use their bodies, for sexual stimulation, and their poetry reflects their effeminacy. This metaphor illustrates as literally as

[40] K. Reckford, pp. 480–481.

[41] *Sonat hic,* in domo divitum. Nam canes lacessiti conantur r literam minitabundi exprimere; idem facturos divites ait, si verum audiant.

Sonat hic, in the homes of the rich. For dogs, when aroused, make the sound of the letter *r* as a threat; and he says that the rich will do the same if they hear the truth.

[42] William S. Anderson, "Persius 1. 107–110," *Class. Quart.* 58 (1958): pp. 195–197.

possible the theme of the Satire, that style is the man. Persius develops this metaphor, first, by equating the poets verbally with their poetry and, second, by establishing patterns of imagery which either relate poetry to parts of the anatomy or describe it as food or sexual stimulus.

The first indication to the reader that Persius intends more than mere literary criticism appears in the adjective *turbida* (5), and the warning *nec te quaesiveris extra* (7). The scholiast's gloss on *turbida* is misleading: *Ab aqua translatio; vel quod multis gentibus repleatur* (A metaphor suggesting water; or because it [Rome] is filled with many races). It is much more likely that Persius here appropriates the Stoic use of this adjective to describe the soul enslaved to passion; as applied to Rome it recalls Socrates' comparison between the parts of the city and the human soul.[43] The phrase *nec te quaesiveris extra* does not mean "do not seek a true judgment of your poetic ability from the mob," but rather "do not seek self-knowledge from the opinions of others." [44] Because the poet's verse reflects his personality, a false judgment of his poetry is also a false assessment of his character. The disturbed state (*turbida*) of Rome's soul renders its judgment false. Several lines later the adversary explicitly states the key metaphor when he asks: *ten cirratorum centum dictata fuisse / pro nihilo pendes?* (Does the fact that you have been dictated to a hundred curly-headed schoolboys carry no weight with you? 29–30). Persius deliberately phrases the question in this way to emphasize that the poet and his poetry are one; he may therefore be said to be dictated. Conversely in line 51 it is the poem, rather than the poet, which is drunk with hellebore. A few lines later the adversary says, *verum . . . amo, verum mihi dicite de me* (I love the truth, tell me the truth about myself, 55).[45] Although on one level the speaker may be asking for opinions of his verse, Persius uses the personal pronoun *me*, just as earlier he used *te* (7), to express the dominant metaphor that literary criticism implies criticism of character.

[43] *Repub.*, IV.435b ff., 445c; V.449. Cf. Cicero, *Tusc. Disp.* III.10.23, IV.10.24, and Seneca, *Epis.*, CIV.22, CXIV.3, where *turbida* is used in a related context.

[44] G. Albini, ed., *A. Persii Flacci Saturarum Liber* (Imola, 1907), and Nino Scivoletto, ed., *Auli Persi Flacci Saturae* (Florence, 1956), translate *te* as the object of *extra*, but most editors either interpret the phrase generally to mean "shun popular recognition," or take it to refer to literary criticism. There is no reason, however, why *te* cannot be the direct object of *quaesiveris* and *extra* an adverb.

[45] Cf. Trimalchio's request to his guests, *Satyr.*, 78: *Fingite me mortuum esse. Dicite aliquid belli* (Pretend I'm dead. Say something nice).

The climax to these obvious equations of the poets with their poetry occurs in Persius' mock recantation: *nil moror. euge omnes, omnes bene, mirae eritis res* (I will hold back no longer. Bravo! Excellent! You are all wonderful! 111). The phrase *mirae eritis res* is a colloquial expression which may be loosely translated as "you are all miracles of perfection" (Gildersleeve) or "everybody's incomparably wonderful" (Merwin).[46] On another level, however, *res* also has the more precise meaning of "poetic subject matter" and the phrase as a whole serves as the final and most explicit statement of the dominant metaphor of the Satire.[47] It also suggests a new interpretation of the opening line of the Satire: *O curas hominum! o quantum est in rebus inane!* (O the cares of men! How empty are their concerns!). As an echo of Lucretius this line hints that Persius' Satires, like the *De rerum natura*, will offer men philosophical guidance.[48] But on another level, through the play upon the meaning of *res*, this line denounces the empty (*inane*) subject matter of modern poetry, the emasculated poets. It therefore forms an appropriate introduction to the entire Satire.

Persius also develops several patterns of imagery based upon the dominant metaphor. He frequently compares poetry to food (*escas*, 22, *fermentum*, 24, *sartago*, 80) or associates it with food (30–31, 51, 53, 97, 125) to suggest its physical appeal to an appetite of the body. He also relates poetry to different parts of the anatomy (*pulmo*, 14, *guttur*, 17, *ocello*, 18, *lumbum*, 20, *iecore*, 25, *nare*, 33, *palato*, 35, *linguas*, 81, *cervice*, 98, and *labris*, 105). Similarly the reading public is often described physically as *auriculis* (22, 108), *cirratorum* (29), *os populi* (42), and *calve* (56). To associate the poets' poetry with their lack of virility Persius refers to this poetry by neuter indefinites (*aliquid*, 14, *quiddam*, 33, *siquid*, 34, *quidquid*, 52, *quidnam*, 98, and *hoc*, 105). The descriptions of this poetry are

[46] Basil Gildersleeve, ed., *The Satires of A. Persius Flaccus* (New York, 1875), p. 99; W. S. Merwin, tr., *The Satires of Persius* (Bloomington, 1961), p. 61. Cf. Petronius, *Satyr.*, 58.12: *bella res est volpis uda*, and 58.13: *bella res et iste qui te haec docet* (lit. "A wet fox is a pretty thing" and "a pretty thing is he who teaches you these manners." Both expressions are highly ironic).

[47] Persius himself uses *res* in this way earlier in the Satire when the adversary says: *sive opus in mores, in luxum, in prandia regum / dicere, res grandes nostro dat Musa poetae* (Whether he treats of the morals and excesses of the age, or the banquets of kings, the Muse gives our poet noble subject matter, 67–68). It is also significant, I think, that the word *res* falls in the line immediately following the exact middle of the poem, line 67; cf. *supra*, p. 19.

[48] Hendrickson (1928a), pp. 97–100. Cf. Lucretius, I.330, 569, II.14. According to the scholion on Lucilius, I.9 (Marx, ed. [Leipzig, 1904–1905]), Persius borrowed this line from the earlier satirist.

also filled with words connoting softness and effeminacy: *mobile, fractus* (18), *plorabile* (34), *tenero* (35, 98, 107), *eliquat* (35), *molli* (63), *fluere* (64), *leve* (64, 82), *laxa* (98), *saliva* (104), and *natat* (105). In addition, Persius alludes several times to the loss of virility in contemporary society (18, 36, 87, 103). In contrast, he employs strong, sharp words to describe the kind of poetry and attitudes which he admires: *uncis* (40), *caedit, demorsos* (106), *mordaci, radere* (107), *secuit* (114), *fregit* (115), *tangit* (117), and *excusso* (118).

The fullest statement of the dominant metaphor, however, occurs in Persius' description of a typical poetry recitation (15–21). The point of this description, that the poets use their poems as they use their bodies, to arouse the sexual passions of their audience, has frequently been obscured by critical misunderstanding of the four lines which follow it:

> P.: tun, vetule, auriculis alienis colligis
> escas,
> auriculis quibus et dicas cute perditus
> "ohe"?
> A.: "quo didicisse, nisi hoc fermentum et
> quae semel intus
> innata est rupto iecore exierit caprificus?" [22–25]

Do you, old man, collect tidbits for the ears of others, ears to which you, corrupt as you are, would cry, "Enough!"?

"What's the point of learning, unless this passion born within me, like leavening or the hardy fig tree, bursts through my heart?"

The antecedent of *quibus* is *auriculis* rather than *escas*, as Housman conjectures;[49] here as elsewhere Persius refers to the audience by an anatomical term, repeating it for emphasis. In the opinion of most editors Persius here imitates Horace, *Ser.*, II.5.96–98, in which Tiresias urges Ulysses to flatter his patron obsequiously:

> importunus amat laudari: donec "ohe, iam!"
> ad caelum manibus sublatis dixerit, urge,
> crescentem tumidis infla sermonibus utrem.

Boor that he is, he loves to be praised. Until he throws up his hands and cries, "Enough now!" ply him with praise, inflate his growing belly with swollen words.

According to this interpretation, in line 23 Persius visualizes the literary patron and amateur poet bursting from the applause of

---

[49] Alfred E. Housman, "Notes on Persius," *Class. Quart.* 7 (1913): p. 14. Clausen (ed. 1956), following Madvig, emends the second *auriculis* to *articulis*, an emendation which I do not believe is necessary. Reckford, p. 477, discusses this point at greater length.

his clients. Despite the plausibility of this explanation it is difficult to believe that in the middle of a complex description Persius would introduce such a relatively weak image and one so unrelated to the imagery preceding and following it. It is more likely that Persius continues the dominant sexual imagery established in the previous lines.[50] The exclamation *ohe* proverbially indicates satiety, here sexual satiety, while the phrase *cute perditus,* which may be translated "sexually corrupt," alludes to the adversary's homosexuality.[51] Martial offers a parallel use of *cute: Pedicatur Eros, fellat Linus: Ole, quid ad te / de cute quid faciant ille vel ille sua?* (Eros is a pederast, Linus practices fellatio; what do you care, Olus, what each one does with his own "skin"? VII.10.1–2).[52] If this interpretation is correct, Persius accuses his adversary of arousing more sexual stimulation in his audience than he, despite his depravity, could endure. The *et* modifies *cute perditus* in the sense of "although," and the entire phrase heightens the hyperbole; the stimulation is so great that it would arouse even a homosexual beyond control.[53]

This interpretation is strengthened by the unusual image of the fig tree which Persius introduces at this point. The two conventional attributes of the fig tree, its barrenness and its ability to push through rocks, particularly tombs, make it an appropriate symbol of bad poetry.[54] But the fact that Persius specifically mentions one kind of fig, the *caprificus* or goat fig, suggests that this detail is im-

---

[50] Cf. the scholion on *Titos:*

Ingentes autem Titos dicit generaliter Romanos senatores a Tito Tatio Sabinorum rege, aut certe a membri virilis magnitudine dicti Titi.

By "great Tituses" he refers either to the Roman senators descended from the Sabine king Titus Tatius, or very likely those called Titus from the great size of their genitals.

Villeneuve, *Les Satires de Perse* (Paris, 1918), pp. 25–26, comments, "It is not impossible, on the other hand, that the word "Titus" had become in vulgar Latin a kind of nickname with a meaning well-suited to the crudity of this passage . . . ," and he quotes the scholion.

[51] The expression *ohe, iam satis est* is proverbial and comprehensible without reference to Horace. Cf. Plautus, *Stichus,* 732, *Casina,* 248, and Martial, IV.89.1, 9. Persius probably had the Horatian passage in mind, however, because he borrows Horace's metaphor of words as food (cf. *escas*), and gives it a sexual twist.

[52] For this meaning of *cutis,* see *Thes. Ling. Lat.,* IV, 1578.

[53] Merwin translates (ed. 1961), p. 56: "Dirty old thing, concocting temptations for the ears / Of others, now that you're poxed, shrivelled, and past it!" The sense is close, but the adversary is barren because he is a homosexual, not because he is an old man; *vetule* seems to me metaphorical rather than literal.

[54] The Romans erroneously believed that the *caprificus* was barren; in fact, any fig, properly fertilized, will produce fruit.

portant, and Pliny offers a reason. In his discussion of the goat fig he says:

Caprificus vocatur e silvestri genere ficus numquam maturescens, sed quod ipsa non habet alii tribuens, quoniam est naturalis causarum transitus aeque ut e putrescentibus generatur aliquid [*Hist. Nat.,* XV.211.79].

The name *caprificus* [goat fig] is given to a species of wild fig which never matures, but which gives to another fig what it does not have itself, since it is quite natural in the course of events for something to be generated from decaying matter.

The process which Pliny refers to in the phrase *sed quod ipsa non habet alii tribuens* is called caprification, or pollination by *blastophagae,* an insect commonly found in goat figs. Pliny imagines that these insects fly from the wild *caprificus* to the cultivated fig and, as they eat the latter's fruit, they let in the sun and air which fertilize this fig.[55] Persius must have been familiar with this idea for he uses the fig to symbolize poetry which, arising from a barren source (the homosexual poet), arouses the productive sexual urges of its audience, the *ingentis Titos* (20).[56] Instead of being merely obscure, this image summarizes the meaning of the previous lines and is therefore extremely relevant to the context in which it occurs. This metaphor suggests, in turn, that the other images in the Satires merit equally close examination before being dismissed as unnecessarily complex.

Verbal and rhetorical devices complement the imagery in this Satire. Verbal repetition, for example, offsets positive and negative values, the ideal and the real. Instead of biting their nails over revisions of their poetry (*sapit unguis,* 106), the poets sound like preaching uncles (*sapimus patruos,* 11). The false praise (*euge,* 49), compared with well-deserved applause (*euge, poeta,* 75), underscores the differences between good and bad poetry, and when Persius mockingly repeats the word later (*euge, omnes,* 111), its false ring is clearly audible. Similarly, Persius uses *ponere* to contrast two worthless actions, serving a dinner as a bribe for praise (*ponere*

[55] Pliny's knowledge of botany is scanty; in reality, when the male flowers of the *caprificus* are placed among the female flowers of other figs, the *blastophagae* crawl out of the *caprificus* to lay their eggs, carrying with them the pollen to fertilize the female figs. Pliny's error does not, however, affect the reference in Persius.

[56] Although the *ingentis Titos* could refer solely to homosexuals, the analogy to the *caprificus* suggests that the poet's audience includes virile aristocrats whose sexual impulses are aroused by this kind of verse. In keeping with his key metaphor identifying the poet and his poetry, Persius here transfers the barrenness of the poet to his verse and compares it to the *caprificus.*

sumen, 53) and devising rhetorical figures (*posuisse figuras,* 86), with the poets' true task (*ponere lucum,* 70). The same point is made in the repetition of *Romulidae saturi* (30) and *rus saturum* (71). And, finally, in the last part of this Satire Persius effectively compares the writers he admires with the kind of audience he disdains by several conspicuous repetitions (*ludit,* 117, *ludere,* 127, *fregit,* 115, *fregerit,* 130, and *vafer,* 116, 132).

In many respects the prologue and the first Satire are similar. In each Persius adopts the persona of the rebellious young writer, critical of the poetic Establishment, who urges his fellow poets to forsake Greek models and draw upon their own literary tradition. Furthermore both poems criticize the same group of people, the contemporary poets, and if one interprets the prologue as an attack, not upon Nero, but more generally upon the aristocrats who encourage their clients to applaud and imitate their inferior verse, the adversary in the first Satire certainly represents these aristocrats. Yet there are significant differences in the attitudes of the speakers in these poems. The poet of the prologue, publishing his artistic manifesto, sounds more arrogant; he places greater emphasis upon his own role as a Roman writer and perhaps for this reason he is highly critical of respected poets, like Ennius, who imitated the Greeks. The poet of the first Satire, on the other hand, is less aggressive, more inclined to laugh at his contemporaries, and slightly more tolerant: he admires Old Comedy and even approves of certain early Roman authors, such as Accius and Pacuvius, who were greatly influenced by the Greek dramatists. The similarity between the two poems seems to me a strong argument for the authenticity of the prologue and, as I hope to show through comparison with the other Satires, the technical skill evidenced in the first Satire, and to a lesser extent in the prologue, points to a late date for both poems. Several classical poets, after completing a book of verse, wrote prefatory poems which in the published *libellus* introduced their other works and Persius, I suggest, followed this procedure. As the first Satire progresses, moreover, the speaker seems to become more impatient until toward the end of the poem his manner approaches that of the poet in the prologue. Perhaps after finishing the first Satire Persius wrote the prologue to give vent to the indignation generated in that poem.

CHAPTER THREE

SATIRE II

In his second Satire Persius does not appear to have completely mastered the poetic techniques which he handles so skillfully in the first Satire. The poem as a whole lacks unity, the adversary is a shadowy figure who never answers his opponent directly, and the solemn didactic tone is unrelieved by the humor evident in the first Satire. Comparison of the two Satires suggests that the second was written before the first and possibly represents an early effort. If we accept the testimony of the *Vita* that Persius began writing satire *mox ut a schola magistrisque devertit,* and if with Villeneuve we include his study with Cornutus in this period, we may attribute the technical weaknesses and fervent tone of this poem to Persius' artistic inexperience and recent preoccupation with Stoicism.[1]

The close connection between the fourth Satire and the pseudo-Platonic dialogue, *Alcibiades* I, has led commentators to speculate that Persius also read and imitated its companion piece, the *Alcibiades* II, in the second Satire. Toward the end of the Greek work Socrates says of the gods:

οὐ γάρ, οἶμαι, τοιοῦτόν ἐστι τὸ τῶν θεῶν, ὥστε ὑπὸ δώρων παράγεσθαι οἷον κακὸν τοκιστήν. . . . καὶ γὰρ ἂνν δεινὸν εἴη, εἰ πρὸς τὰ δῶρα καὶ τὰς θυσίας ἀποβλέπουσιν ἡμῶν οἱ θεοί, ἀλλὰ μὴ πρὸς τὴν ψυχήν, ἄν τις ὅσιος καὶ δίκαιος ὢν τυγχάνῃ [149e].[2]

---

[1] Villeneuve (1918a), p. 177.

[2] The adjective *seductis* (4) appears to echo παράγεσθαι and the phrase *ius fasque* (7) recalls the Greek ὅσιος καὶ δίκαιος. Nicola Terzaghi, *Per la storia della satira* (2nd ed., Messina, 1944) Appendix: "Persio, Sat. 2 e l'Alcibiade II," pp. 155–159, believes that although the Greek dialogue contributed the idea that one should let the gods decide what to give, the image of Juppiter in the poem and the motif of praying for riches in secret derive from the Cynic diatribes.

I do not think that it is the nature of the gods to be influenced by gifts, like the evil money lender . . . for it would be strange if the gods paid attention to a man's gifts and sacrifices but not to his soul, as to whether it was just and holy.

This remark may have suggested to Persius the theme of his Satire, but since he is primarily interested in the corruption of religion by avarice he ignores the theme of the Greek dialogue, that through ignorance one may utter harmful wishes, and focuses instead upon the mercenary quality of men's prayers.

The Church fathers admired the Christian overtones of this Satire, particularly the apostrophe, *O curvae in terris animae et caelestium inanis* (O, souls bowed to earth and empty of divinity! 61), but the humorless severity of the Stoic speaker alienates most modern readers. Yet to criticize Persius, as some editors have, because he lacks Horace's genial nature is to overlook the fact that Horace's persona is completely unsuited to Persius' purpose in this poem. Both writers were equally critical of their contemporaries but they chose different ways of expressing their criticism: Horace plays the role of a close friend, aware of his own faults, who always has his reader's best interests at heart, whereas Persius, in this Satire at least, assumes the more impersonal role of an indignant Stoic philosopher. This persona differs sharply from that of the flippant young poet in the first Satire; he is older, more didactic, and less indulgent toward his adversary.[3] He shuns the familiarity of the first person but does not hesitate to use himself as an example of correct behavior; he would not let others pray for him (39–40), and he alone knows how to worship with a pure heart (71–75). Furthermore, he reveals only a cynical, ironic sense of humor when he asks his adversary: *heus age, responde (minimum est quod scire laboro) / de Iove quid sentis?* (Come now, tell me—I'm asking only one small question—what are your feelings toward Juppiter? 17–18), or when he wryly acknowledges the profits of the flesh: *peccat et haec, peccat, vitio tamen utitur* (It sins and sins, yet benefits from vice, 68). Although we may find this persona too stern and unsympathetic to be convincing, it is the most appropriate one to deliver the Stoic diatribe which Persius presents, and to the Greek or Roman reader the criterion of a successful persona was whether or not it suited the author's subject

[3] The distinct personalities of these two speakers refute Witke's assertion (1962), p. 153, that Persius has only one persona. Cf. *supra,* p. 17.

matter.[4] Certainly this Stoic commands respect and if he inspires resentment he at least compels our attention by the vigor of his condemnation.

Through this persona Persius attacks the religious hypocrisy of his contemporaries, particularly the Roman aristocrats who held positions of moral authority. To indicate that he is singling out these men he changes the Horatian phrase, *at bona pars hominum* (*Ser.*, I.1.61), to *at bona pars procerum* (5) and directs his remarks to a fictional representative of this group. His handling of the adversary, however, indicates that at this stage in his career Persius was absorbed in the philosophic themes he was presenting and did not yet realize the advantages to be gained through vivid dialogue and fully developed characters. The adversary thus plays a completely passive role and has little physical or social identity but his religious views are carefully delineated. His first secret wish, *o si / sub rastro crepet argenti mihi seria dextro / Hercule!* (O if only, by Hercules' favor, a pot of silver would rattle against my hoe! 10–12), betrays his stupidity, for he echoes an imaginary prayer of Horace which the latter hopes he will never be foolish enough to repeat.[5] The adversary's other requests for legacies (10, 12–13), larger herds, and more land (46, 49) confirm his avarice and materialistic attitude toward prayer. His concept of the gods is also archaic and degrading; he forms them in his own fallible image (18–22, 52–56) and superstitiously believes in omens and rituals which his hypocrisy renders meaningless (15–16, 24–27, 44–45, 48–49, 55–56). Through these details Persius portrays his opponent's mental state but certainly does not make him an interesting character.[6]

Like Satire I, the second Satire begins and ends with two short sections complementing each other and contrasting with the rest of the poem.[7] The opening lines to Macrinus appear at first to have little relevance to Persius' theme; they describe a rather insignificant good luck ritual in a light, informal manner which differs sharply from the Stoic's later fervent moralizing. Yet there

[4] Cf. J. F. d'Alton, *Roman Literary Theory and Criticism* (repr., New York, 1962), pp. 116–127, and the original sources cited therein.

[5] Horace, *Ser.*, II.6.8–13. V. d'Agostino, "La seconda satira di Persio e 'l'auri sacra fames'," *Convivium* 1 (1929): p. 575, notes a similar wish in Petronius, *Satyr.*, 88.

[6] I do not believe it is necessary, however, to argue as Villeneuve does (1918a), pp. 323–326, that there are several different adversaries in this poem.

[7] Cf. *supra*, p. 27.

is, I think, an important connection between these lines and the rest of the poem. Whereas most men pray to the gods in secret (*seductis divis,* 4, *tacita acerra,* 5) and ask for future gifts, Macrinus openly thanks the gods for the fortunate year which has passed. The adjective *candidus,* in addition to its literal meaning of "white," is often used metaphorically to mean "frank" or "sincere." [8] Here, I believe, Persius evokes this double association to underscore the sincerity of Macrinus' gesture. A few lines later he reiterates this point through the contrast of *tacita acerra* (5) and *aperto voto* (7), each occupying the same place in the line. Finally, in the closing lines of the poem the Stoic translates Macrinus' individual gesture into a general precept:

> quin damus id superis, de magna quod dare
> lance
> non possit magni Messalae lippa propago:
> conpositum ius fasque animo sanctosque
> recessus
> mentis et incoctum generoso pectus honesto.
> haec cedo ut admoveam templis et farre litabo [71–75].[9]

Instead let us offer to the gods above things which the bleary-eyed off-spring of great Messala cannot offer on his great platter: justice and reverence blended in the soul, holiness in the recesses of the mind, and noble integrity imbued in the heart. Allow me to carry these to the temple and I will make a favorable sacrifice with grain.

Like the opening lines of the Satire, these lines emphasize the importance of giving (*damus*) from a pure heart (*animo, mentis, pectus*); to make the connection even clearer, the verb *litabo* echoes the earlier *libabit* (5), while the phrase *admoveam templis* recalls the words *tollere de templis* (7).[10]

Apart from the link between these two passages, however, the second Satire does not exhibit the same kind or degree of unity found in the other Satires, perhaps because it is an early work. In these other Satires Persius uses a façade of spontaneous conversation to conceal the logical argument, but behind this façade

---

[8] For examples of this figurative use of *candidus,* see Ovid, *Epis. ex Pont.,* IV.14.43, Velleius, II.116.5, Seneca, *Suas.,* VI.22, Petronius, *Satyr.,* 107, Pliny, *Epis.,* II.9.4. The adjective *merum,* while referring primarily to undiluted wine, also reinforces the image of purity in these lines.

[9] I do not agree with Wendell Clausen (ed. 1956), p. 13, that lines 71–72 are a question and prefer to follow Owen's punctuation here.

[10] In effect the opening lines of this Satire establish positive values against which Persius develops his negative view of contemporary religion. Anderson (1960b), pp. 66–81, shows how skillfully Persius employs this same technique in *Sat.,* V.1–51.

a logical argument *does* exist, augmented usually by a dominant metaphor and a coherent pattern of images and verbal repetitions. In this Satire the logical connections between the separate sections are less obvious and there is no dominant metaphor unifying the whole.[11] Instead Persius develops his theme, that effective worship requires complete harmony between one's external and internal being, by contrasting inner purity and external cleanliness, piety and materialism, and frankness and secrecy.[12]

We have already seen the latter contrast stated in the opening lines of the poem (*candidus*, 2, and *aperto voto*, 7, vs. *seductis divis*, 4, and *tacita acerra*, 5). The Stoic's next remark, *haut cuivis promptum est murmurque humilisque susurros / tollere de templis* (Hardly anyone is ready to carry his murmurings and low whispers outside the temples, 6–7), reiterates this contrast by implicitly urging the adversary to voice his prayers aloud in public. The latter's wishes reveal the conflict between his external and internal self; ironically, he prays aloud for spiritual improvement (*mens bona, fama, fides*, 8) and secretly for external possessions (*introrsum, sub lingua*, 9). The Stoic's comment on these prayers introduces the second contrast between inner purity and external cleanliness: *haec sancte ut poscas, Tiberino in gurgite mergis / mane caput bis terque et noctem flumine purgas?* (Do you plunge your head two or three times into the Tiber in the early morning to purge away the night, so that you may make your requests with a pure heart? 15–16).[13] If the adversary prays for evils such as wealth,

---

[11] Villeneuve (1918a), p. 322, attempts to analyze the logical structure of Persius' argument but his conclusions are not particularly helpful. He divides the Satire into four parts: lines 5–30, discussing men's foolish prayers and false conceptions of the gods; lines 31–40, which treat women's superstitious vows and thus contrast with the previous section; lines 41–51, pointing out that sacrifices annul the prayers themselves; and lines 52–75, attacking the false notion that the gods love gold. According to Villeneuve, Persius first criticizes the assumption that any prayer is acceptable if accompanied by the proper ritual. He then shows how these rituals destroy the efficacy of these vows and, finally, he argues against the debased concept of deity underlying such prayers. D'Agostino, p. 574, follows Villeneuve's divisions.

[12] Reckford, p. 488, calls the theme of this poem "the contrast between shadow and substance," but he does not discuss the Satire in great detail.

[13] I disagree here with Clausen (ed. 1956), p. 11, who does not punctuate these lines as a question. The scholiast's explanation of this ritual, *lotus propterea quod nocturno coitu sis inquinatus* (washing because you are stained with nightly intercourse), is undoubtedly correct; cf. Kirby F. Smith, *The Elegies of Albius Tibullus* (New York, 1913), p. 242, for a list of parallels. It seems odd, however, that in that case the adversary dips only his head rather than his entire body into the Tiber. The latter detail suggests to me another level of

the Stoic implies, he cannot acquire inner purity simply by performing a ritual of purification. The Stoic later echoes this theme when he describes the superstitious old woman (*avia aut metuens divum matertera*, 31) who performs a similar purifying ritual over a child (*lustralibus ante salivis / expiat*, 33–34), and then fatuously prays that he, too, may be wealthy:

> nunc Licini in campos, nunc Crassi
>   mittit in aedis:
> "hunc optet generum rex et regina, puellae
> hunc rapiant; quidquid calcaverit hic,
>   rosa fiat" [36–38].[14]

---

interpretation. Since the adversary later praises the gods *somnia pituita qui purgatissima mittunt* (who send dreams cleansed of phlegm, 57), perhaps here he is attempting to clear his head from an excess of phlegm, for which Celsus, IV.5.4, recommends dousing the head with water:

> Quo vitio levato, si in destillatione crassa facta pituita est, vel in gravedine nares magis patent, balneo utendum est, multaque aqua prius calida, post egelida fovendum os caputque. . . .

> Once the illness has lessened, if there remains a thick flow of phlegm, or, in the case of a cold, if the nostrils are open, one should take a bath in a great deal of water, first hot then cool, and douse the face and head.

Horace twice uses *pituita* to symbolize an impediment to the virtuous life, once facetiously when he puns upon the meaning of *sanus* and refers to the Stoic *sapiens* as *praecipue sanus, nisi cum pituita molesta est* (particularly wise, unless he is bothered by phlegm, i.e., has a cold, *Epis.*, I.1.108), and once seriously when he describes the effects of overeating:

> dulcia se in bilem vertent stomachoque tumultum
> lenta feret pituita. Vides ut pallidus omnis
> cena desurgat dubia? quin corpus onustum
> hesternis vitiis animum quoque praegravat una
> atque adfigit humo divinae particulum aurae [*Ser.*, II.2.75–79].

Rich food turns to bile and heavy phlegm raises havoc in the stomach. Do you see how pale each one looks as he leaves the smorgasbord? In fact, the body, staggering under yesterday's excesses, drags the mind down with it and pins to earth this particle of the divine spirit.

Horace's use of *humo* parallels Persius' phrase *humilisque susurros* (6, cf. 61 and *infra*, p. 46). Furthermore Cicero, *Tusc. Disp.*, IV.10.23, compares the soul controlled by depraved opinions to the diseased body *cum sanguis corruptus est aut pituita redundat aut bilis* (when the blood is diseased and there is an excess of phlegm or bile). If these passages have any bearing on lines 15–16, the Stoic's question acquires added significance; invoking the Stoic correlation of physical and spiritual disease, he implies that his adversary's congested head symbolizes his inability to think rationally and that even if he clears his head he will not thereby clarify his thinking.

[14] The phrase *rex et regina* in a Roman context sharply emphasizes the fairy tale quality of these prayers noted by Ludwig Friedländer, *Roman Life and Manners Under the Early Empire* (London, 1913) 4: p. 90. W. R. Halliday, "Persius, II.37," *Class. Rev.* 38 (1924): p. 169, believes that these verses recall "blessing invoked by singers of seasonal songs upon members of the household," but the modern Greek parallels which he cites are unconvincing.

Now she sends him off to the estates of Licinus and the mansions of Crassus. "May some king and queen desire him for a son-in-law, may all the girls pursue him; and wherever he walks, may roses bloom."

The old woman's clean white garments (*albata*, 40) do not guarantee her inner purity and, as Seneca explains in a letter to Lucilius, the prayers of these guardians are particularly harmful to a child:

Etiamnunc optas quod tibi optavit nutrix tua aut paedagogus aut mater? Nondum intellegis quantum mali optaverint? O quam inimica nobis sunt vota nostrorum! eo quidem inimiciora quo cessere felicius. Iam non admiror si omnia nos a prima pueritia mala secuntur; inter execrationes parentium crevimus [*Epis.*, LX.1].[15]

Do you still want the things which your nurse or tutor or mother wished for you? Don't you realize how evil their wishes were? How dangerous for us are our family's prayers! The more propitiously they turn out, the more dangerous they are. Indeed, I am not surprised that all our misfortunes stem from early childhood, for we are raised amidst our parents' curses.

The adversary's prayers and concept of the gods, compared with the Stoic's prayer at the end of the poem, illustrate the contrast between true piety and materialism. The adversary asks to increase his material possessions (10–11, 45–46, 49–50), he does not believe that Juppiter is aware of his actions unless the latter sends a visible omen (24–27), and he gilds the gods' statues because he assumes they share his admiration for gold (55–58). These details revealing the adversary's concern with the externals of religion contrast vividly with the Stoic's prerequisites for true piety: *conpositum ius fasque animo sanctosque recessus / mentis et incoctum generoso pectus honesto* (73–74). The verbs in this couplet point to another series of contrasts developed in this Satire. According to the Stoic the religious person gives to the gods (*damus, dare,* 71) a heart in which *ius, fas,* and *honor* are completely blended together and harmonized (*conpositum, incoctum*). Here Persius associates the concepts of giving and adding or blending with true piety; elsewhere in the Satire he associates their opposites, receiving and subtraction or destruction, with religious hypocrisy. Despite the abstract quality of these concepts, they are developed in concrete examples. The religious hypocrite in the poem continually prays

---

[15] Cf. *Epis.*, XXXI.3:

Surdum te amantissimis tuis praesta; bono animo mala precantur. Et si esse vis felix, deos ora ne quid tibi ex his quae optantur eveniat.

Remain deaf to your loved ones' prayers, for despite their good intentions they ask for harmful things. And if you wish to be happy, beg the gods not to let their prayers come true.

to receive things *from* the gods (*da . . . da*, 45–46, *dabitur*, 50), and makes requests instead of giving thanks (*poscis*, 3, 15, 41, *rogarit*, 40). The adversary also hopes to dig up buried treasure (11), or strike the heir ahead of him out of a will (*expungam*, 13); the oak struck by Juppiter's lightning is torn from the ground (*discutitur*, 25), and the adversary's guilty heart shakes out drops of sweat (*excutiat*, 54). These images of subtraction and destruction reoccur when the Stoic argues that the demands of his flesh force man to violate the world around him:

> haec sibi corrupto casiam dissoluit
>   olivo,
> haec Calabrum coxit vitiato murice vellus,
> haec bacam conchae rasisse et stringere
>   venas
> ferventis massae crudo de pulvere iussit [64–67].

The flesh spoils olive oil, mixing it with cinnamon, and dyes Calabrian wool with harmful purple hues; the flesh orders man to tear the pearl from the oyster and bids him strip the veins of glowing ore from the bleeding earth.

Conington has noted the violence of the verbs in this passage (*dissolvit, coxit, rasisse, stringere*); it is perhaps also significant that this violence changes or corrupts the products of Nature (*olivo, vellus, bacam, pulvere*).[16] Just as the virtuous man, according to the Stoics, lives harmoniously with Nature, so the irreligious man opposes her and tries to destroy or usurp her possessions.

We can see, then, how Persius unifies this Satire to a certain extent by organizing it around a series of contrasts between external appearance and inner reality. Verbal repetition provides an additional degree of unity. The description of men's prayers as *humilis* (6), from the noun *humus* meaning "earth," the old woman's wish for the child, *quidquid calcaverit hic, rosa fiat* (38), the adversary's references to his property (44, 49) and to buried treasure (10–12), and, finally, the allusion to mining (66–67), literally confirm the Stoic's description of men as *curvae in terris animae* (61). In another notable repetition the adversary prays aloud

---

[16] J. Conington and Henry Nettleship, eds., *The Satires of A. Persius Flaccus* (3rd ed., Oxford, 1893), p. 47. The echo in lines 64–65 of Vergil's praise for the farmers who do not alter the products of Nature heightens the relevance of the Stoic's words: *Alba neque Assyrio fucatur lana veneno / Nec casia liquidi corrumpitur usus olivi* (The white wool is not stained with Assyrian dye, nor is the olive oil spoiled by the addition of cinnamon, *Geor.*, II.465–466). It is also interesting that the items mentioned in Persius' lines represent natural products of the field, animals, the sea, and earth respectively.

(*clare*, 8) to improve his character but under his breath he hopes for a *praeclarum funus* (a magnificent funeral, 10) for his uncle. He regards both the heir ahead of him and Juppiter as sources of money and tries to push both around (*inpello*, 13, *inpellere*, 21); similarly, gold has driven out bronze (*inpulit aera*, 59). Persius also compares simple offerings of grain and wine (*merum*, 3, *farre*, 75) with greasy animal sacrifices (30, 44–45, 47–48), and then extends the epithet to gold (*pingui auro*, 52–53). The mercenary quality of contemporary religion is emphasized in the repetition of *emaci* (3) and *emeris* (30), and in the frequent allusions to gold and silver (11, 52–53, 55, 58–59, 69). The differences between true and false piety appear in the contrasts between the *praetrepidum cor* (54) of the adversary and the *incoctum pectus* (74, cf. *coxit*, 65) of the Stoic, between the temple defiled by gold (*sancto*, 69) and the *sanctosque recessus mentis* (73–74), and between *animae curvae* (61) and *conpositum ius fasque animo* (73). But perhaps the most significant verbal echo in the poem is *libabit* (5) and *litabo* (75). The first means merely "to sacrifice," the second, "to sacrifice properly, or with favorable omens"; the difference lies in the sincerity of the Stoic speaker.

Of the six Satires the second is certainly the least successful, technically, and the least appealing to the modern reader. But it is interesting, I think, because it reveals Persius in an experimental stage of his career, when he had not yet settled on the most effective persona to persuade his audience and when he was still searching for the techniques of poetic unity which he handles so adroitly in his later Satires.

SATIRE III

Many of the weaknesses of the second Satire are noticeably absent in the third. The organization is clearer, the individual parts logically related, and the dominant metaphor of disease, physical and spiritual, carefully established through a complex pattern of imagery and verbal repetition. Furthermore the protagonists in this Satire are not such shadowy figures as those in Satire II. Persius' persona, it is true, resembles the didactic Stoic of the previous Satire, even imitating the latter's technique of rapid interrogation, but his personality is more fully developed and the tone of his remarks more varied. Similarly, the adversary, although he speaks only twice in the poem, comes alive through the wealth of concrete detail used to portray his character.

This Satire dramatizes the favorite Stoic analogy between the philosopher who analyzes spiritual illness and recommends Stoicism as a cure and the doctor who diagnoses physical disease and prescribes a regimen. These two situations are causally related: Persius makes it very clear that the cause of the youth's spiritual malady, his dissolute life, is also enervating him physically, and if he does not heed the Stoic now he will later resemble the physically ill fool at the end of the poem. Persius develops this argument in three parts corresponding to the major structural divisions of the Satire. The first section diagnoses the youth's spiritual disease to demonstrate that he needs Stoicism (1–62), the second outlines the concerns of Stoicism and attributes the adversary's hypothetical rebuttal to a centurion (63–87), and the third illustrates the consequences to the youth if he heeds the objections rather than the doctrine (88–118).[17]

In contrast to the hostile persona of the second Satire, Persius here plays a friend of the adversary, a Stoic who tries to persuade him to resume his neglected study of philosophy. To the distress of several editors, however, Persius does not maintain this role consistently in the beginning of the poem but instead alternates it with that of an impersonal narrator. This inconsistency, as well as the similarity between Persius' background and that of the adversary, convinced A. E. Housman that the first section of the Satire was an interior monologue between Persius' higher self, represented by the Stoic, and his lower self, represented by the dissolute youth.[18] Kenneth Reckford accepts Housman's theory, calling it "sensitive, profound, tempting," and adds: "The resemblance to the author of the person corrected rather than the corrector is an Horatian indirection, a placation of the reader through ironic self-criticism, and a refusal to accept full responsibil-

---

[17] In view of the close logical relationship between all three parts of the poem, it is difficult to agree with George Hendrickson, "The Third Satire of Persius," *Class. Phil.* 23 (1928): pp. 340–342, that the last thirty lines do not belong to the Satire. Hendrickson argues that these lines do not illustrate the theme of the poem, the folly of recognizing virtue and ignoring it, but he infers from the scene between the doctor and the sick man (88–106) that if the latter had obeyed the doctor he would have been cured. This seems to me a clear illustration of the theme as Hendrickson defines it, and I do not see the illogicality of these lines.

[18] Housman (1913), pp. 16–18.

ity for any sermon as such. Undoubtedly, Persius considered the avoidance of dogmatism a prerequisite of sincerity." [19] While several critics agree with Housman, even those who dissent often equate Persius with his persona and assume that lines 44–51 describe a true incident from his childhood.[20]

As I suggested earlier, the biographical approach to Roman satire is of doubtful value and in the third Satire raises more problems than it solves. There is a simpler explanation for Persius' alternation of roles. This device allows him to involve us, his audience, in the poem, thereby including us in his criticism of the youth.[21] To accomplish this Persius first establishes a deliberate ambiguity between the narrator's remarks to us and the Stoic's words to his sleeping adversary. Finding ourselves *in medias res* as the Satire opens, we are drawn into the poem through the verb *stertimus* (we snore, 3), and are encouraged to identify with the youth; our resentment is then anticipated and, through the use of *credas* (you would think, 9), we become bystanders in a formal scene between the adversary and the Stoic. The introduction of the dramatic framework at this point is particularly effective because it allows Persius to continue criticizing us while at the same time it encourages us to relax our defenses in the belief that someone else is the victim. Thus the Stoic includes us as well as the adversary in the verbs *querimur* (12, 14) and *venimus* (16), and since the narrator addressed us earlier in the second person (*credas*, 9), the Stoic's remarks to the adversary in this person also apply to us. Significantly, once Persius has established in our minds the similarity between ourselves and the indolent youth, he discards the persona of the narrator and maintains that of the Stoic philosopher throughout the rest of the poem.[22]

Because he frequently varies the tone of his criticism and uses himself as an example, this Stoic persona is much more persuasive than his counterpart in the second Satire. His humorous hyperbole of the youth bursting with rage and braying like a donkey is

---

[19] Reckford, pp. 495–496.

[20] Nicola Terzaghi, "La terza satira di Persio," *Scritti per il XIX centenario dalla nascità di Persio* (Volterra, 1936): p. 88; Ciaffi, pp. 71–72, 90–91; R. Verdière, "Notes critiques sur Perse," *Collec. Latomus* 23 (1956): p. 343. Cf. *supra*, p. 6.

[21] Witke (1962), p. 156, discussing Persius' use of this technique in the prologue, maintains that "in the ability thus to weave the audience into the poem, the genius of Persius resides."

[22] I believe that the Stoic imagines the scene in lines 88–97 and so plays the role of both doctor and patient; cf. *infra*, p. 57.

calculated to win the reader's goodwill and establish a receptive mood for criticism. In line 15 the tone sharpens as the Stoic, now serious, derides his adversary, comparing him to a helpless bird and a spoilt child (16–17). He then tempers these accusations by momentarily assuming the adversary's viewpoint:

> . . . Sed rure paterno
> est tibi far modicum, purum et sine labe salinum
> (quid metuas?) cultrixque foci secura patella [25–26].

You have a small family estate with a modest yearly crop, a spotless salt-cellar (why should you worry?), and an offering dish, the carefree guardian of the hearthside shrine.

The ironic *quid metuas,* however, anticipates the change in mood which follows as the Stoic turns on his adversary, attacking his ancestral pride and suggesting that he is a second Natta:

> non pudet ad morem discincti vivere Nattae.
> sed stupet hic vitio et fibris increvit opimum
> pingue, caret culpa, nescit quid perdat, et alto
> demersus summa rursus non bullit in unda [31–34].

You are not even ashamed to live like sloppy Natta; yet his vices leave him in a stupor, his body is growing fat and soft, he lacks all sense of guilt and doesn't even know what he is losing, and he has sunk so deep that he does not even send up a bubble.

In passing, the Stoic carefully justifies his role as critic: *ego te intus et in cute novi* (I know you from within, beneath the skin, 30).

The climax to this sermon, the apostrophe to Juppiter (35–38), attests to the Stoic's sincerity and religious conviction. The following lines then offset this didactic moralizing with a vivid scene from the Stoic's own childhood. Whether or not this scene reflects Persius' own youth is immaterial; what is important is that here the Stoic appeals to his own experience to persuade. By conceding his youthful lack of interest in philosophy and preference for childhood games, he wins our sympathy so that we listen more willingly to his precepts; and by implying that, unlike his adversary, he gave up these childish pleasures for Stoicism, he gains our respect.[23]

After this brief interlude the Stoic again attacks his adversary, this time climaxing his argument with an emotional appeal to all men to follow Stoicism (66–72). This serious exhortation is

---

[23] To emphasize his childhood dislike of Stoicism, the Stoic humorously refers to his teacher as *non sanus.* Villeneuve (1918b), p. 268, overlooks the irony when he argues that since only the Stoic *sapiens* was truly *sanus,* the epithet is just. The reference to Cato's dying words (45) confirms the fact that it was a Stoic discourse which the child was avoiding.

in turn balanced by the centurion's humorous picture of philosophers:

> obstipo capite et figentes lumine terram,
> murmura cum secum et rabiosa silentia
>   rodunt
> atque exporrecto trutinantur verba labello,
> aegroti veteris meditantes somnia: gigni
> de nihilo nihilum, in nihilum nil posse
>   reverti [80–84].

With bowed heads and eyes glued to the ground they chew on their own mumblings and mad silences, weighing words on outstretched lips. They ponder the dreams of some sick old man, that nothing is born from nothing and nothing returns to nothing.

This passage is doubly ironic, however, for in his confusion between Epicureanism and Stoicism the centurion betrays his total ignorance.

The final section of the Satire presents a scene within a scene. The conversation between the Stoic and his youthful adversary, which began as a semi-dialogue but quickly turned into an extended monologue, resumes in line 107 and forms the larger dramatic framework for a scene between a patient and his doctor (88–106). By introducing this hypothetical scene and assuming the role of the doctor (as well as the patient), the Stoic encourages a comparison between himself and the physician. This comparison is strengthened in turn by the patient's epithet for the doctor, *sodes* (89), and his warning, *ne sis mihi tutor,* both of which recall the earlier reference to the Stoic as the youth's *comes* (7). In refusing to argue with the sick man (*perge, tacebo,* 97), the Stoic emphasizes the latter's stubborn nature, and the epic parody of *Aen.,* VII.84 in line 99, as well as the ironic *beatulus* (103), heighten the satire.

In the final scene with the adversary the Stoic again assumes a condescending tone, underscored by the use of the first person plural (111–114), but he is careful to retain the reader's goodwill at the end by a diverting play on words:

> nunc face supposita fervescit sanguis
>   et ira
> scintillant oculi, dicis facisque
>   quod ipse
> non sani esse hominis non sanus iuret
>   Orestes [116–118].

Now when the fire is kindled your blood boils and your eyes gleam with wrath and you say and do things which Orestes, himself insane, would swear were the doings of a madman.

It is clear, I think, that the Stoic in this poem is more persuasive than his companion in the second Satire because he draws upon his own experience and consistently varies the tone of his discourse.

Through an abundance of concrete detail Persius also creates a vivid adversary. When we first see him he is sleeping off a night of heavy drinking; upon waking he imperiously calls for his slaves and, when no one answers, flies into a rage (8–9). His anger, excessive drinking, and later his inability to dilute his writing ink (12–14), all reveal a lack of self-control. His aristocratic background perhaps increases his tyrannical disposition; the Stoic mentions his Tuscan ancestry and *rure paterno* (24), implying that he lives off a moderate patrimony and does not bother to support himself. He is interested only in such status symbols as rank, clothing, and material possessions (27–29, 73–76), and although he once studied Stoicism he has long since neglected it (52–59). Unlike his friend he refuses to grow up and continues his childish pursuits (17–18, 61–62). This indolent youth is also indirectly characterized by the Stoic's later reference to the *torosa iuventus* (86), the foolish young men who lower themselves to join the centurion in deriding philosophy. The adversary convicts himself most eloquently, however, when he comments on the imaginary scene between a patient and his doctor: unable to perceive the close relationship between spiritual and physical illness, he assumes that he is healthy because he has no chills or fever, and he turns a deaf ear to his friend's warnings. In his obtuseness he resembles the poetaster of the first Satire, but he does not defend himself as vigorously as the latter.

The dominant metaphor in this Satire plays upon the literal and figurative meanings of *sanus,* "healthy" and "sane." Persius' treatment of this Stoic commonplace recalls his technique in the second Satire; starting with the concepts of knowledge and health versus ignorance and disease, he relates other pairs of abstractions to these concepts. Softness, pliancy, lack of control, and gluttony are associated with ignorance and disease, while hardness, purposefulness, self-control, and the simple life accompany knowledge and good health. These abstractions are expressed in concrete images and the contrasts between them reiterated through verbal repetition.[24] To illustrate how these devices unify the Satire, I have incorporated the discussion of them in a systematic reading of the poem.

[24] Reckford, p. 489, n. 2, gives a partial list of these repetitions which I have included in my discussion.

The Satire opens with a description of sunlight penetrating a darkened room, an image which evokes the metaphorical association of light and knowledge, ignorance and darkness. Since it is the Stoic's task to educate the adversary, this image serves as a keynote for the entire poem. The adversary is then introduced still sleeping off the excesses of the night before; as I noted above, his drinking suggests his lack of control, here emphasized by the adjective *indomitum* (3). His companion's first words, *en quid agis? siccas insana canicula messes / iam dudum coquit et patula pecus omne sub ulmo est* (What are you doing? The mad dog star has long since been parching the dry fields and the whole herd has sought shelter under the spreading elm, 5–6), do more than inform the adversary poetically that it is past noon; they also warn him of his illness. To the Greeks and Romans the dog star (*canicula*), here aptly described as *insana*, heralded disease and often coincided with the crisis of an illness;[25] thus it is not surprising that soon after this warning the spiritual malady afflicting the youth comes to a symbolic crisis and he bursts with rage: *turgescit vitrea bilis: / findor, ut Arcadiae pecuaria rudere credas* (The vitreous bile swells up inside him: "I am bursting!" he brays, like a herd of Arcadian asses, 8–9).[26]

A series of striking images confirms the adversary's malleability and loss of control. He is compared to a soft dove (16), a spoilt child (17), a leaky vessel (20),[27] and in a particularly effective image, to damp clay: *udum et molle lutum es, nunc nunc properandus et acri / fingendus sine fine rota* (You are soft, damp clay; now, now you must quickly be molded on the endlessly spinning wheel, 23–24). These lines imply that the adversary still has an opportunity to reform, for unlike the vessel which has already been fired when a flaw is discovered and therefore cannot be repaired, the youth's character is not yet molded.[28]

---

[25] Cf. Hippocrates, *Airs, Waters, Places*, XI.

[26] H. Lackenbacher, "Persius und die Heilkunde," *Wien. Stud.* 55 (1937): pp. 130–141, discusses the medical allusions in the Satires but overlooks this example.

[27] This comparison recalls Persius' earlier use of the verb *despumare* (3), a term borrowed from wine-making which refers to the process of skimming off the lees from new wine; cf. Vergil, *Geor.*, I.295–296. In the present context it implies an apt comparison between the drunken youth and a vessel filled with new wine.

[28] Persius' phrase *non cocta* is ambiguous; I prefer to translate it "insufficiently fired" rather than "unfired," since a vase in the leather-hard stage would not resound sharply. This interpretation accords with the scholiast's gloss, *non bene coctum* (not properly baked).

The Stoic's allusions to the adversary's possessions further de-
lineate his character; the phrase *sine labe salinum* (25) recalls the
earlier image of the youth as a leaky vessel (20), while the adjective
secura, here modifying *patella* (26), is later applied to the adversary
himself (62). Both phrases suggest the importance of self-knowledge,
the theme of the next section (30–62). Natta's slovenly appearance
(*discincti,* 31) betrays his equal lack of self-control, but unlike the
adversary who knows from his study of philosophy how he should
live, Natta is not even aware of his error *(nescit,* 33), and, ironically,
will never suffer the spiritual torment facing the adversary. The
torments mentioned represent acute physical pain (the Sicilian
bull), potential physical pain (the sword of Damocles), and spiritual
agony (the guilty conscience). The order is ascending; spiritual
anguish exceeds all physical pain.

Through verbal repetition the Stoic makes it clear to the
adversary that this suffering awaits him. The allusion to tyrants (35)
recalls the youth's earlier despotic behavior, *similis regum pueris* (17).
The adjective *ferventi* (37) anticipates the lust which later grips the
adversary (*fervescit sanguis,* 116), while the verb *terruit* (41) answers
the earlier question *quid metuas?* (26). Furthermore the pallor
induced by the guilty conscience (*palleat,* 43) is later paralleled
by several allusions to paleness accompanying physical illness
(85, 94, 96). Finally, the verb *nesciat* (43) links this passage both
to the preceding description of Natta (33) and to the subsequent
example of forgivable ignorance (*scire,* 49).

In much the same way the Stoic establishes significant parallels
between himself as a child and the adversary (44–51). The child
dabs his eyes with oil to induce temporary blindness (here also
used metaphorically), so that he may avoid a Stoic declamation;
the adversary's eyes burn with an un-Stoic wrath (*scintillant oculi,*
117), which blinds his reason. The child tries to avoid throwing the
canicula (singles) on the dice (49), while the adversary is warned
of his growing illness by the presence of the dog star (5). Yet while
the child prays that he may win in competition (*scire erat in voto,*
49), the Stoic, now mature, prays that tyrants may acknowledge
virtue (35–38); this last detail, taken together with other parallels,
implies that the Stoic, unlike the adversary, eventually exchanged
his childhood interests for worthier Stoic goals.[29]

[29] *Tangebam* (4, 37, 107), *discere* (46, 66, 73), *summum* (34, 48), *dexter* (57,
107), *grandia* (45, 55), *raderet* (50, 114), *angustae* (2, 50), *orcae* (50, 76).

The Stoic then compares his ignorance as a child with the adversary's knowledge of Stoicism, a comparison analogous to the one made earlier between Natta and the man who recognizes virtue. The child does not know the outcome when he twists his top (*torquere*, 51), but the adversary knows how to distinguish twisted habits (*curvos mores*, 52) from correct ones; yet unlike the earnest Stoic who lives on beans and stays up all night studying (54–55), the adversary gorges himself into a stupor and sleeps all day (58–59). The verb *stertis* recalls the earlier *stertimus* (3), while *laxum*, *soluta*, and *dissutis* echo previous references to the adversary's pliant nature. The final image of him wandering aimlessly, throwing shards at crows, epitomizes his complete lack of purpose.

The first sixty-two lines of this Satire thus demonstrate conclusively that the adversary is suffering from a spiritual malaise. The second section announces a cure in a passage uniting the literal and figurative aspects of the dominant metaphor and occurring, significantly, soon after the middle of the poem:

> elleborum frustra, cum iam cutis aegra
> > tumebit,
> poscentis videas; venienti occurrite morbo,
> et quid opus Cratero magnos promittere
> > montis?
> discite et, o miseri, causas cognoscite
> > rerum:
> quid sumus et quidnam victuri gignimur,
> > ordo
> quis datus, aut metae qua mollis flexus
> > et unde,
> quis modus argento, quid fas optare,
> > quid asper
> utile nummus habet, patriae carisque
> > propinquis
> quantum elargiri deceat, quem te deus
> > esse
> iussit et humana qua parte locatus es
> > in re [63–72].[30]

You may see men calling in vain for hellebore when the sickly skin is already swelling; meet the illness on the way and then why should you have to promise Craterus mountains of money? Learn, o miserable men, to recognize the causes of things: what we are and what kind of life we are allotted; what the starting order is, and when and where to make the gentle turn around the goal post; what constitutes a moderate sum, and what it is proper to pray for; what uses new money has, and how

---

[30] Cf. *supra*, pp. 19, 34, n. 47.

much one should give to one's country, family, and relatives; what sort of person God wants you to be, and where your place is in the human community.

Here the cure for what appears to be a physical ailment turns out to be Stoicism. The hypothetical scene in the first two lines relates the earlier picture of the adversary shouting for his attendants and bursting with anger to the later one of the patient summoning his doctor (88–89). Furthermore, the Stoic's apostrophe recalls his original question, *o miser inque dies ultra miser, hucine rerum / venimus?* (O miserable man, growing worse by the day, have we come to this? 15–16), for his enumeration of Stoic concerns begins and ends with the word *res*.

Since the argument of the Satire reaches a logical conclusion at line 76, one may justly ask why Persius did not end the poem here instead of adding several more scenes and characters. The answer, I think, is that Persius wished to strengthen the Stoic's argument by showing the adversary what would happen if he ignored his friend's advice. Persius' choice of a foolish centurion as a spokesman for the opposition serves a twofold purpose: since the soldier, like the adversary, scorns intellectual pursuits, Persius uses him to criticize the adversary indirectly, but at the same time the centurion's ignorance is so obvious that the adversary can flatter himself by comparison.[31] The centurion's opening remark, *quod sapio satis est mihi* (What I know is enough for me, 78), touches upon the theme of knowledge versus ignorance and recalls the Stoic's previous question to the adversary, *hoc satis?* (Is this enough? 27). The centurion also echoes the adversary's lack of interest in philosophy (*non curo,* 78, cf. 26, 62), and his impressions are diametrically opposed to the truth. Whereas Persius has already suggested metaphorically that philosophy illuminates ignorance (*extendit lumine rimas,* 2), the centurion accuses the philosophers (again metaphorically) of keeping their knowledge to themselves (*figentes lumine terram,* 80). He adds that they ponder the dreams of a sick man,[32] grow pale over their studies, and stop eating, yet the man who ignores Stoicism turns pale, becomes sick, and eventually dies after a heavy meal. Despite

[31] Furthermore, the adversary, unlike the centurion, may still be persuaded to return to philosophy. The Stoic therefore tactfully does not undermine his own persuasive arguments by attributing these objections to the adversary, for to do so would be to insult his intelligence.

[32] Cf. J. W. Spaeth, "Persius on Epicurus: A Note on Satires 3.83–84," *Trans. Amer. Philol. Assoc.* 73 (1942): pp. 119–122.

his confusion between Stoicism and Epicureanism, however, the centurion wins the approval of imaginary bystanders, the *torosa iuventus* (86). These figures appear instead of the adversary because the latter has not yet completely rejected Stoicism and the Stoic wishes to illustrate the kind of person he will resemble if he agrees with the centurion. By recalling the earnest young students of Stoicism (*detonsa iuventus,* 54) in the phrase *torosa iuventus,* the Stoic emphasizes the disparity between them.

The introduction of a brief dramatic scene at this point illustrates more vividly than pure description ever could the grim fate awaiting the youth if he does not heed the Stoic's advice. The clay color of the sick man's skin evokes the earlier image of the youth as damp clay (*lutea,* 95, *lutum,* 23), and the references to swelling and turgidity suggest the adversary bursting with rage (*surgit,* 95, *turgidus,* 98, *turgescit, findor,* 8–9). The sick man also emulates the adversary's gluttony and dies from overeating *inter vina* (100). Verbal repetition heightens the irony of his death; his body is arranged on a funeral couch (*conpositus,* 104, cf. 91), and he is smeared with unguents (*lutatus,* 104, cf. *lutea,* 95).

The adversary's reaction to this scene confirms that he has been present as the Stoic painted this imaginary picture, but failing to understand he derisively addresses the Stoic by the latter's epithet for him, *miser* (107, cf. 15, 66). In his reply the Stoic taunts the youth for having a soft mouth (*tenero in ore,* 113), just as earlier he compared him to a soft dove which eats only predigested food (*teneroque columbo,* 16).[33] He further reminds him of his resemblance to the dead man through the iteration of *albus* (98, 115) and *excussit* (101, 115). And, finally, after recalling several earlier warnings through additional repetitions, he concludes by referring twice in the same line to the word which serves as the dominant metaphor for the entire Satire, *sanus* (118).[34]

[33] Lackenbacher, p. 138, notes that Celsus, II.1.18, associates mouth ulcers with physical weakness: *Si qua inbecillitas oritur, proximum est, ut infantes tenerosque adhuc pueros serpentia ulcera oris . . . exerceant* (If some weakness arises, it is very likely that ulcers spreading in the mouth are bothering infants and young children).

[34] Cf. *molle* (23, 68, 110), *putre* (114, *putet,* 73), *radere* (50, 114), *deceat* (71, 114).

CHAPTER FOUR

SATIRE IV

In his 1605 edition of Persius' Satires, Isaac Casaubon, after pointing out the numerous verbal echoes in the opening lines of this Satire and the Greek dialogue, *Alcibiades I,* remarked at line 22:

Ab hoc versu quae deinceps sequuntur omnia usque ad illa verba non longe a fine

—ilia subter
caecum vulnus habes—(43–44)

neque commune quicquam habent cum dissertatione Socratis apud Platonem; neque proprie ad Alcibiadem aut ad Neronem spectant.[1]

Everything after this verse up to those words shortly before the end— "beneath the groin you nurse a hidden wound"—is entirely unrelated to Socrates' discourse in Plato's dialogue; nor do these lines refer to Alcibiades or Nero.

Later commentators have generally accepted Casaubon's statement without asking whether a closer relationship exists between the two works or how well known this Greek dialogue and others like it were to Persius and his contemporaries. The answers to these questions, I believe, shed light upon Persius' intention in the fourth Satire and justify consideration of these Greek prototypes, their transmission to Rome, and their influence upon Persius. The material summarized here is discussed in greater detail in the Appendix.[2]

The *Alcibiades I* belongs to the literary genre of *Sokratikoi*

---

[1] I. Casaubon (ed. 1605), p. 337. Casaubon identified Alcibiades with Nero in this Satire.

[2] In this discussion of the Greek sources of the fourth Satire I am indebted to Professor Friedrich Solmsen of the University of Wisconsin Institute for Research in the Humanities for many helpful suggestions. He is in no way responsible for any errors of interpretation.

logoi. The term is Aristotle's and refers to the dialogues portraying Socrates which were composed after his death by several of his students and admirers, among them Plato, Xenophon, Antisthenes, and Aischines.[3] Unfortunately, aside from those of Plato and Xenophon most of these *Sokratikoi logoi* have disappeared completely or exist only in fragments. A particularly popular form was the conversation between Alcibiades and Socrates, a type probably arising in response to the *Katēgoria Sokratous* of Polykrates (*ca.* 393/2–387 B.C.), which cited Alcibiades as the foremost example of Socrates' dangerous influence upon Athenian youth.[4] Diogenes Laertius names Plato (*Alcibiades I, II*), Xenophon, Antisthenes, Aischines, Phaidon, and Eucleides as authors of *Alcibiades* dialogues and implies that several others existed, but of these only the *Alcibiades I* and *II* and a few fragments of Aischines are extant.[5] Like the *Alcibiades I,* Aischines' dialogue appears to have discussed the qualities necessary for a good statesman; furthermore, both conversations closely resemble the Euthydemus dialogue preserved in Xenophon's *Memorabilia* in which, as Dittmar and Gigon have pointed out, Euthydemus is substituted for Alcibiades.[6] It would be unwise to conclude on the basis of these similarities that all of the lost *Alcibiades* dialogues conformed to this same general pattern,[7] but since Polykrates blamed Alcibiades' political career upon Socrates, we may reasonably assume that some of the *Alcibiades* dialogues discussed statesmanship, perhaps along similar lines. A comparison of the extant remains reveals the general

---

[3] Aristotle, *Poet.*, I.7–9, 1447b; cf. *Rhet.*, III.16, 1317a, and a fragment preserved in Athenaeus, XI.505c (V. Rose, ed., *Aristotelis qui ferebantur librorum fragmenta* [Leipzig, 1886], p. 78, no. 72). E. M. Cope, *The Rhetoric of Aristotle,* rev. by J. E. Sandys (Cambridge, 1877) 3: p. 192, interprets the phrase *Sokratikoi logoi* to include other dialogues besides Plato's, and relates it to Horace, *Carm.*, I.29.14 and III.21.9, and *Ars Poet.*, 310; cf. Appendix, pp. 103–104. V. de Magalhães-Vilhena, *Le Problème de Socrate* (Paris, 1952), pp. 346–347, agrees with Cope and adds, p. 330: "In addition it is a special form of the prose dialogue with its own setting, characters, and characteristic themes; it is a literary genre with its own principles, rules, and artistic conventions." Cf. the same author's *Socrate et la légende platonicienne* (Paris, 1952), p. 65.

[4] De Magalhães-Vilhena (1952b), pp. 39–40. See also George C. Field, *Plato and His Contemporaries* (London, 1930), pp. 133–174, on these dialogues.

[5] Diogenes Laertius, II.61, 64, 108; III.51; VI.18.

[6] H. Dittmar, *Aischines von Sphettos,* Philol. Untersuch. 21 (Berlin, 1912), p. 127; Olof Gigon, *Kommentar zum ersten Buch von Xenophons Memorabilien,* Schweizer. Beitr. zur Altertumsw. 5 (Basel, 1953), p. 40, and the same author's "Xenophontea," *Eranos Rudbergianus* 44 (1946): p. 150.

[7] Some, for example, may have discussed religion along the lines of the *Alcibiades II.*

outlines of this type of dialogue (see Appendix). Alcibiades is presented as a young man who believes that his rank and beauty raise him above other men; he further boasts of knowing the nature of justice and goodness without having been taught. Socrates proves to him that he is completely ignorant and no better than a slave or a lower class citizen (*dēmiourgos*). To emphasize his inferiority, Socrates may even compare him to other Greek or Oriental leaders. When Alcibiades perceives his true state he feels ashamed and perhaps weeps; he asks Socrates how he may be cured and is told that self-knowledge (*gnōthi sauton*) and caring for oneself (*epimeleia heautou*) are essential.

In the Hellenistic period the *Sokratikoi logoi* seem to have been widely read in philosophic circles and after they were brought to Rome, probably by Panaetius in the second century B.C. (see Appendix), they circulated among the educated reading public through the first century A.D. and beyond.[8] Undoubtedly Persius had read some or all of these works, for beside the fact that he was an ardent Stoic his imitation of the *Alcibiades I* in the fourth Satire indicates a close familiarity with the Greek original. Most commentators point out the verbal echoes between the two works in the first twenty-two lines of the Satire,[9] but none has noticed the more important similarities in structure. Both works begin with a reference to Alcibiades' ambition to be a politician (1, *Alc.* I, 105b, 106c), and mention his external endowments. In the Greek dialogue Socrates lists his family, physical attractiveness, and precocious knowledge (104a–b, 110c); in the fourth Satire the order is reversed and the reference to Alcibiades' family and beauty delayed until line 20, but the details are similar. Following this exposition, Socrates demonstrates to his pupil in the *Alcibiades I* that he does not know the nature of justice, injustice, good, or evil (109b–117b). His major argument is that Alcibiades could not have acquired this knowledge from the mob as he claims because although men and states can agree about objective facts,

---

[8] Interest in the *Alcibiades* dialogues continued through the sixth century A.D. In the second century, besides Aelius Aristides, Maximus Tyrius was also familiar with Aischines' *Alcibiades* (Dittmar, pp. 97, 115–117); in the following century Libanius probably read these dialogues before composing his defense of Socrates, and in the fifth and sixth centuries, respectively, Proclus and Olympiodorus both wrote commentaries on the *Alcibiades I*, which they considered an excellent introduction to Platonic philosophy.

[9] Several commentaries, including those of Villeneuve and G. Némethy, ed., *A. Persii Flacci Satirae* (Budapest, 1903), quote these verbal reminiscences in full.

they do not agree about the nature of abstract concepts or value judgments (111c–112d). Later in the conversation, as an example of an objective fact agreed upon by individuals and states, Socrates mentions numbers which are obtained by measurement or by the use of a balance (126d). Taken together these two passages imply that measuring instruments cannot settle disputes over justice and injustice, moral right or wrong. Persius seems to have composed lines 10–11 of his Satire with these passages in mind, even borrowing the images of the ruler and scale from the Greek original. As a result, although Persius' Socrates appears on the surface to acknowledge Alcibiades' wisdom, he in fact reveals the youth's total ignorance. Lines 10–13 thus correspond to the demonstration of ignorance in the *Alcibiades I*, 109b–117b. Similarly, Persius' allusion to hellebore, the cure for insanity (16), echoes Socrates' description of Alcibiades' political plans as a μανικὸν . . . ἐπιχείρημα (a mad undertaking, 113c).

To avoid limiting the pertinence of his Satire by dating it historically, Persius omits most of the next section of the *Alcibiades I* which discusses the Persian *paideia* (120–124c). He does, however, allude to the final part of this section in line 20, where the picture of Alcibiades boasting of his superiority, *"Dinomaches ego sum,"* *suffla, "sum candidus"* ("I'm the son of Dinomache"—puff yourself up—"I'm the fairest"), recalls a similar scene in the Greek dialogue in which Alcibiades, called ὁ Δεινομάχης υἱός (the son of Deinomache, 123c), challenges the Persian king. Persius then compares Alcibiades to an old herb seller, Baucis (21–22). These lines translate poetically the motif noted earlier in the *Alcibiades* dialogues, the comparison between Alcibiades and the *dēmiourgos* who lacks self-knowledge. In the *Alcibiades I* this comparison does not follow the section on the Persians, as Persius' order might indicate, but instead occurs much later, toward the end of the dialogue (131a). In Aischines' *Alcibiades,* however, a similar comparison may have concluded Socrates' discussion of Themistocles which, as Dittmar remarks, corresponds to the passage on the Persians in the *Alcibiades I*. If so, Persius perhaps here follows Aischines rather than the *Alcibiades I* in introducing the comparison at this point.[10]

Contrary to the opinion of most of Persius' commentators, I do

[10] This conjecture assumes that Cicero's description of Alcibiades weeping (*Tusc. Disp.,* III.32.77) is drawn from Aischines' *Alcibiades* and reflects the sequence of ideas in the latter work: (1) Socrates proves to Alcibiades his ignorance, (2) Socrates compares him to *dēmiourgos* (*baiolum*), and (3) Alcibiades weeps. I suggest also that the allusions to Baucis and *baiolum* (instead of the

not believe that the imitation of the *Alcibiades I* ends here at line
22. In the latter, after discussing the Persians Socrates alludes
briefly to the maxim *gnōthi sauton* (124b), and then turns to the
theme of *epimeleia heautou*. He argues that this does not mean
concern for the possessions of others or one's own possessions
or even one's body, but concern for the soul, self-knowledge (124b–
131a). The man who cares only for his body, the money maker, and
the lover are cited as examples of men who lack self-knowledge
because they care for their possessions rather than their souls (131b–
c). As we might expect, Persius' Satire follows the same sequence of
ideas. After a brief reference to self-knowledge (23–24), Persius
introduces three figures who illustrate the wrong kinds of *epimeleia*:
the miser Vettidius who cares only for his possessions, the narrator
of the anecdote who cares only for the possessions of others, and
the homosexual who cares only for his body (25–41). Persius then
returns to the theme of self-knowledge and in conclusion alludes
to two of the three examples cited by Socrates, the money maker
(47, 49) and the lover (48).[11] These structural similarities clearly
suggest that Persius' entire fourth Satire is a close imitation of
the *Alcibiades I*.

In addition to these similarities, however, there are also significant differences in the two works due to their different purposes.
The Greek dialogue uses logical argument to reveal a moral vice
(self-deception), and offers a remedy before it is too late. Hence
Alcibiades can be shown before he has begun his political career,
thereby manifesting his ignorance, and while he can still correct
his faults. As a satirist, however, Persius needs an obvious vice
to satirize and so he introduces Alcibiades after he has entered
politics and his corruption by the people has already begun.[12]
This change may also explain a second difference between the

---

closer translation of *artifex*) share a specificity which may denote a common
source, one which perhaps compared Alcibiades to a stock figure representative
of the *dēmiourgoi*. This source may have been Aischines. Cf. Appendix, pp.
102–103.

[11] The corresponding reference in the *Alcibiades I* to the money maker
(131c) supports the interpretation of line 49 as a reference to usury. Both
Némethy (ed. 1903), pp. 232–233, and Villeneuve (1918b), pp. 108–109, offer
lengthy analyses of this passage.

[12] Casaubon (ed. 1605), p. 319, first noted this difference without giving the
reason for it, yet it is appropriate, I think, to the apologetic purpose of the
Alcibiades dialogues that Alcibiades be shown before his career has advanced
to the point where Socrates' advice is useless, and that he appear to heed
Socrates, if only temporarily.

two works, the emphasis upon homosexuality in Persius' Satire. The idea is present in Socrates' warning to Alcibiades toward the end of the Greek dialogue:

τοῦτο τοίνυν αἴτιον, ὅτι μόνος ἐραστής ἦν σός, οἱ δ'ἄλλοι τῶν σῶν. τὰ δὲ σὰ λήγει ὥρας, σὺ δ'ἄρχῃ ἀνθεῖν. καὶ νῦν γε ἂν μὴ διαφθαρῇς ὑπὸ τοῦ 'Αθηναίων δήμου καὶ αἰσχίων γένῃ, οὐ μή σε ἀπολίπω. τοῦτο γὰρ δὴ μάλιστα ἐγὼ φοβοῦμαι, μὴ δημεραστὴς ἡμῖν γενόμενος διαφθαρῇς. πολλοὶ γὰρ ἤδη καὶ ἀγαθοὶ αὐτὸ πεπόνθασιν 'Αθηναίων. εὐπρόσωπος γὰρ ὁ τοῦ μεγαλήτορος δῆμος 'Ερεχθέως· ἀλλ' ἀποδύντα χρὴ αὐτὸν θεάσασθαι. εὐλαβοῦ οὖν τὴν εὐλάβειαν ἣν ἐγὼ λέγω [132a].[13]

This, then, is the reason why I alone was your lover while all the others loved your body. Yet your body is starting to fade while you are beginning to bloom. Even now, unless you are corrupted by the people of Athens and become ugly, I will never desert you. I fear this most of all, that you may become the people's lover (*dēmerastēs*) and be corrupted; many good Athenians have already suffered this fate. For the mob of magnanimous Erechtheus has a fine face, but you should see it naked. Therefore take my advice and be discreet.

The epithet *dēmerastēs* and the personification of the *dēmos* as a handsome man whose nakedness reveals his physical corruption both suggest homosexuality. In the fourth Satire this becomes the dominant metaphor: Alcibiades is a *dēmerastēs* whose relationship to the *populi* is, metaphorically, a homosexual one. Finally, a third difference concerns Socrates' tone and manner in each work. In the *Alcibiades I* Socrates only occasionally employs irony, preferring for the most part to address Alcibiades sympathetically and lead him through dialectic to the realization of his own ignorance. In Persius' Satire, on the other hand, Socrates is primarily a critic whose most effective weapon is irony. Undoubtedly irony plays a major role in this poem because it was traditionally associated with Socrates, but I suggest also that it serves to relieve the didactic tone of the Satire.[14] A consideration of Persius' persona will clarify this point.

In the very beginning of the poem, as in the first Satire, Persius acknowledges the device of the persona: *"Rem populi tractas?"*

---

[13] Plutarch perhaps had this passage in mind when he described Socrates' concern for Alcibiades (*Alcib.*, IV.1), because he even includes the flower image implicit in the verb ἀνθεῖν in the *Alcibiades I*. Persius also alludes to this image in the phrase *marcentis vulvas* (36); as Némethy notes (ed. 1903), p. 227, "A flower is properly said to wilt."

[14] Cf. G. C. Fiske, *Lucilius and Horace*, Univ. of Wis. Stud. in Lang. and Lit. 7 (Madison, 1920), pp. 100–104. Persius, of course, does not imitate true Socratic irony as Horace, for example, does. Because Alcibiades' vices require a much more caustic weapon, Persius deliberately sharpens the irony to the point of bitter sarcasm.

(*barbatum haec crede magistrum / dicere, sorbitio tollit quem dira cicutae*) ("Are you handling the people's affairs?"—imagine these are the words of the bearded teacher carried off by an unlucky draught of hemlock, 1–2). From these opening lines to the end, the poem is a virtual monologue delivered by Socrates. This places an added burden upon the satiric persona, for besides describing the adversary in full, he must also persuade without becoming didactic. In the second Satire neither of these problems is satisfactorily solved, but here in the fourth Satire Persius has created in Socrates an effective persona for the monologue. Admittedly Socrates does not have a strong individuality in this Satire nor does he refer to his own life or experiences. Instead he represents a manner of argument. If this seems surprising at first, one must remember that in antiquity the details of Socrates' life were overshadowed by his importance as the originator of a manner of argument characterized by irony and indirection. I use the word "manner" here to distinguish these devices from Socrates' dialectic method. In the Platonic dialogues, since they concern the discovery of truth, dialectic and the ironic manner complement one another, while in Persius' Satire, which criticizes rather than discovers vice, the ironic manner becomes more important than dialectic.

Because it is indirect the Socratic manner of argument is particularly suited to offset the didactic quality latent in the satiric monologue. In the fourth Satire Socrates employs three forms of indirect criticism: first, he is consistently ironic and therefore ambiguous; second, he attributes his most severe criticism to anonymous speakers; and, third, he prefers indirect to declarative statements. The first of these devices, irony, develops gradually throughout the poem. Although he introduces his description of Alcibiades (4–13) with an ironic *scilicet,* Socrates deliberately restrains his irony in the beginning to deceive Alcibiades into thinking that he agrees with him and concedes his superior knowledge. He then turns on him in lines 14–16, one of the few direct attacks in the poem, and from the harshness of his words we realize that his previous remarks were completely ironic (10–13). Another effective use of irony occurs in lines 33–41, where the deliberately shocking description of Alcibiades sunning himself is underscored by the casual manner in which Socrates introduces it:

> at si unctus cesses et figas in cute solem,
> est prope te ignotus cubito qui tangat et acre

despuat: "hi mores! penemque arcanaque lumbi
runcantem populo marcentis pandere vulvas.
tum, cum maxillis balanatum gausape pectas,
inguinibus quare detonsus gurgulio extat?
quinque palaestritae licet haec plantaria vellant
elixasque nates labefactent forcipe adunca,
non tamen ista filix ullo mansuescit aratro."

But if you are relaxing and oiling your body to catch a bit of sun, a perfect stranger is at hand to tap you on the elbow and sputter savagely: "What kind of behavior is this? Plucking your penis and private parts to spread open your shrivelled vulva to people passing by! Why, when you comb the perfumed beard on your chin, does your prick stand out smooth shaven from your loins? Even if five wrestlers should root out those young shoots and make your flaccid buttocks quiver with their forceps, no plough could tame those ferns."

The words *at si* and *ignotus* establish an ironic contrast between this scene and the previous one in which Alcibiades, initiating the conversation, had asked someone if he knew Vettidius and received a denunciation of the man in reply. Here, Socrates implies, Alcibiades is quietly minding his own business when a complete stranger comes up and attacks him without provocation. Through these remarks, as well as his later comment on the scene, *caedimus inque vicem praebemus crura sagittis. / vivitur hoc pacto, sic novimus* (We kill and in turn offer our legs to the arrows; thus we live, thus we acquire knowledge, 42–43), Socrates ironically suggests that he too disapproves of this self-appointed censor of private morals. Here his ironic manner culminates in an apparent refusal to judge Alcibiades altogether.

Socrates further avoids criticizing Alcibiades directly by ascribing his own views in the two scenes mentioned above to two anonymous speakers.[15] This is particularly effective in the second scene where the satire is extremely harsh. Elsewhere in the poem Socrates generally eschews direct statements in favor of indirect ones. In lines 14–18 he uses rhetorical questions to imply evil rather than accuse, and in lines 23–24, instead of the usual apostrophe addressed to the reader (cf. II.61, III.66), he voices a general exclamation, *ut nemo in sese temptat descendere, nemo, / sed praecedenti spectatur mantica tergo!* (No one dares to descend into himself, no one! he'd rather watch the pack of faults on the back of the man ahead of him), which, incriminating no one individual, indicts all. Similarly, a number of criticisms are mitigated by concessive or

---

[15] This is one of the uses of the adversary recommended by Aristotle, *Rhet.*, III.17.16.

conditional clauses, such as *da verba et decipe nervos / si potes* . . .
(Speak and deceive your twitching groin, if you can, 45–46), or

> viso, si palles, inprobe, nummo,
> si facis in penem quidquid tibi venit, amarum
> si puteal multa cautus vibice flagellas,
> nequiquam populo bibulas donaveris aures [47–50].

If you grow pale, wretch, at the sight of silver, and spend everything you
earn to satisfy your cock, or if you shrewdly lash the money market for
all it's worth, you will give your thirsty ears to the mob in vain.

In fact only in the last two lines of the Satire does Socrates ad-
monish Alcibiades directly; throughout the rest of the poem his
criticism is indirect, yet because of its indirectness more persuasive.

The dominant metaphor of this Satire compares the politician
to a male prostitute. The opening lines of the poem develop this
metaphor gradually, first hinting at Alcibiades' homosexuality and
his perverted hold over the mob. His effeminacy and youth (*ante
pilos*, 5) contrast with Socrates' masculinity and maturity (*barbatum*,
1).[16] Furthermore he exercises a physical hold over the people suggested by the choice of the expression *rem populi tractas* instead of
the more usual *rem publicam geras*.[17] The word *populi* in place of
the more abstract concept of *res publica* focuses attention upon the
mob, while the verb *tractare* implies manual handling.[18] A few lines
later this image becomes explicit. With a gesture of his hand (*manus*,
8) Alcibiades soothes the burning passions of the mob (*fervet*, 6,
calidae, 7); the image points to the analogy of the homosexual
assuaging his partner.[19]

Having hinted at Alcibiades' relationship to the mob, Socrates
derides his ability to make moral judgments in a passage which, as
we have seen, closely imitates a section of the *Alcibiades I*. Socrates
then asks his pupil:

> quin tu igitur summa nequiquam pelle decorus
> ante diem blando caudam iactare popello
> desinis, Anticyras melior sorbere meracas?
> quae tibi summa boni est? uncta vixisse patella
> semper et adsiduo curata cuticula sole?
> expecta, haut aliud respondeat haec anus. i nunc,

---

[16] Reckford, p. 484. Cf. Villeneuve (1918b), p. 98.

[17] Although the expression *res tractare* does occur (e.g., Cicero, *Ad fam.*, VI.6.3,
De or., I.45.199, and *De rep.*, III.3.4), *res gerere* is a much more common idiom.

[18] Cf. Cicero, *Tusc. Disp.*, V.38.111: *ea quae gustemus, olfaciamus, tractemus,
audiamus* (those things which we taste, smell, touch, and hear).

[19] The phrase *maiestate manus* is doubly ironic since *maiestas*, which commonly refers to the supreme sovereignty of the Roman state, is here applied to
an individual and vested in a sexual gesture.

"Dinomaches ego sum," suffla, "sum candidus." esto
dum ne deterius sapiat pannucia Baucis,
quom bene discincto cantaverit ocima vernae [14–22].

You have groomed your skin to no avail; why don't you stop flaunting your "tail" prematurely before the flattering mob and swallow a stiff dose of hellebore instead? What's your ideal? To live high and preen your hide with never ending sunbaths? That's just what this old woman here would wish. "I'm Dinomache's son"—puff yourself up—"I'm the fairest." So be it; you have no more self-knowledge than wrinkled Baucis when she hawks her aphrodisiacs to the wanton household slave.

The words *pelle, caudam, sorbere,* and *cuticula* continue the pattern of physical imagery established in the opening lines.[20] More important, these lines further develop the key metaphor through two comparisons which have been generally misunderstood. The first, contained in the phrase *blando caudam iactare popello,* is interpreted by the scholiast as a reference to a dog wagging its tail when praised.[21] Most later commentators, however, citing Horace's description of the peacock, *picta pandat spectacula cauda (Ser., II.2.26),* argue that Persius alludes to this bird.[22] Without denying the relevance of these passages I suggest that in addition Persius is here referring to Alcibiades' perverted relationship with the mob, *caudam* being a slang term for *penem.* Horace twice uses *cauda* in this sense *(Ser., I.2.45, II.7.49)* and Cicero, in an interesting letter on Roman prudery, notes the early connection between the two terms.[23] *Iactare* is equally appropriate in this context since it denotes voluptuous display.[24] Because the first eight lines of the Satire imply a homosexual relationship between Alcibiades and the *populi,* this image is not unexpected; furthermore Persius repeats it in two later lines (36, 48), the first of which both Némethy and

[20] Cf. *barbatum* (1), *sorbitio* (2), *pilos, calles* (5), *bile* (6), *animus* (7), *manus* (8). *Calles,* meaning literally, "you are thick-skinned," is particularly ironic in view of Alcibiades' excessive pampering of his skin.

[21] *Translatio est a canibus, qui cum blandiuntur dominis, caudam movent* (The metaphor refers to dogs who, when they are petted by their masters, wag their tail [*sic*]).

[22] Cf. Pliny, *Hist. Nat.,* X.43; Ovid, *Ars Amat.,* I.627–628, *Med. Fac.,* 33–34.

[23] Cicero, *Ad fam.,* IX.22:

Caudam antiqui 'penem' vocabant, ex quo est propter similitudinem 'penicillus.' At hodie 'penis' est in obscenis.

Our ancestors used to call a tail *penis* from which we derive the word *penicillus* (paint brush) because of its resemblance. But today *penis* is considered obscene.

[24] Cf. Cicero's definition of *iactatio* as *voluptas gestiens et se efferens insolentius* (desire exulting and brazenly displaying itself, *Tusc. Disp.,* IV.9.20). Cf. also *Tusc. Disp.,* IV.7.16; Horace, *Ser.,* I.2.85; Juvenal, I.61–62.

Reckford recognize alludes to Alcibiades as a male prostitute.[25]

The second comparison between Alcibiades and an old woman, Baucis, as I pointed out, is inspired by a stock motif of the *Alcibiades* dialogues, the analogy between Alcibiades and the *dēmiourgos* who, lacking self-knowledge, is in a slavish condition (see Appendix). Translating this general comparison into a specific scene of an old woman selling herbs, Persius adds four significant details: *pannucia, bene discincto, ocima,* and *vernae. Pannucia,* meaning "ragged" or "wrinkled," suggests a comparison between Alcibiades' pampered skin and Baucis' wrinkles,[26] but inasmuch as it anticipates *marcentis vulvas* (36), it implies that despite his excessive concern for his body, the effeminate Alcibiades resembles a barren old woman. In addition Baucis sells *ocima,* an aphrodisiac, to a slave described as *bene discincto.*[27] In explaining this epithet several commentators quote a Horatian passage implying that household slaves (*vernae*) are less disciplined than others (*Ser.,* II.6.66). The reference to *ocima,* however, indicates that *discincto* here, as in Satire III.31, connotes moral depravity. In his *Epistle* CXIV.4 and 6 Seneca twice applies this adjective to Maecenas whose loose attire, he says, betrayed his effeminacy. The adverb *bene* suggests deliberate disarray befitting a homosexual who wished to display himself, and such a man is a slave (*vernae*) to his passions.[28] The comparison between Alcibiades and Baucis is therefore extremely apt; just as she sells stimulants to sexually depraved slaves, so Alcibiades sells himself and stimulates the depraved passions of the slavish *populi.*[29]

In the next section (23–41), the descriptions of Vettidius and Alcibiades illustrate two erroneous kinds of knowledge, knowledge of one's possessions and one's body. In addition these lines contrast

[25] Némethy (ed. 1903), p. 227, Reckford, p. 486. Reckford also hints at a connection between lines 15 and 36 when he says, "If *iactare* troubles us, it is because Persius is saving the give-away *pandere* for a more climactic moment (line 36)." Nevertheless Reckford accepts the suggestion that the peacock is referred to and neither he nor, to my knowledge, any other commentator recognizes the image as a sexual one.

[26] Villeneuve (1918b), p. 102, mentions this interpretation only to reject it.

[27] Pliny, *Hist. Nat.,* XX.48: *Ocimum quoque . . . venerem stimulat.* Villeneuve (1918b), p. 102, alludes to this passage in Pliny but prefers to translate *ocima* as "herbs." He also suggests, and then rejects, the translation of *discincto* as "debauched."

[28] Cf. *Alc. I,* 135c.

[29] Reckford, p. 486, is the only critic to grasp the relevance of the allusion to Baucis, but he overlooks the particular significance of *ocima.*

the hard life of the miser with the soft existence of the sybarite. Words connoting hardness and softness emphasize the contrast, while the phrases *iugum pertusa ad compita figit* (he fixes the yoke to the crossroad altar, 28) and *figas in cute solem* (you fix the sun on your skin, 33), each occupying the end of a line, deliberately echo one another.[30] The description of Alcibiades sunning himself finally makes explicit the dominant metaphor. The phrase *populo marcentis pandere vulvas* suggests more than mere exhibitionism. The word *populo*, recalling three earlier references to the rabble of the popular assembly (*populi*, 1, *plebecula*, 6, *popello*, 15), acquires political overtones, while the verb *pandere* suggests prostitution. Most unexpected, however, is the word *vulvas* placed emphatically at the end of the line. This term, as the scholiast notes, refers to female genitalia and as far as I can determine is never applied elsewhere in classical literature to a man.[31] In addition to this clear-cut allusion to Alcibiades' effeminacy, the agricultural imagery in these lines transfers to him the well-known comparison between a woman and a fertile field.[32]

The dominant metaphor also underlies the battle imagery in lines 42–46:

> caedimus inque vicem praebemus crura sagittis.
> vivitur hoc pacto, sic novimus. ilia subter
> caecum vulnus habes, sed lato balteus auro
> praetegit. ut mavis, da verba et decipe nervos,
> si potes. . . .

We kill and in turn offer our legs to the arrows; thus we live, thus we acquire knowledge. Below the groin you nurse a secret wound, unseen beneath your broad gold belt. If you prefer, speak and try to deceive your twitching groin, if you can. . . .

On the battlefield of politics the mob and the politician, through their perverted relationship, mutually destroy each other. The hint of a sexual wound in *crura* and *ilia* is confirmed by the verb *novimus* which, besides referring ironically to the theme of the Satire, the

---

[30] Cf. *iratis* (27), *deradere* (29), *mordens* (30), *aceti* (32) vs. *unctus* (33), *marcentis* (36), *elixas* (40).

[31] Scholion: *Vulvas vero pro natibus posuit multo audacius; nam feminarum loca vulvae sunt* (He very boldly writes "vulvae" for "buttocks," since vulvae are part of the female anatomy). P. Pierruges, *Glossarium Eroticum Linguae Latinae* (Paris, 1826), p. 518, s.v. *Vulva*, cites only this line of Persius and explains it: *pro podice tanquam cunni aemulo*.

[32] Cf. Sophocles, *Ant.*, 569; Plautus, *Asin.*, 873–874, *Truc.*, 147–150, *Curc.*, 36; Lucretius, IV.1107, 1272; Vergil, *Geor.*, III.136; Martial, VII.71.

need for self-knowledge, is a euphemism for sexual intercourse.[33]
Socrates' warning, *da verba et decipe nervos, / si potes,* does not
mean "try to ignore the physical pain of your wound," as Némethy
suggests, but instead refers to the idea that a man's speech betrays his
character.[34] As we have seen, the first Satire develops this theme more
fully, again using the homosexual as an example of the man who
does not know himself and advising that self-knowledge lies within
oneself: *nec te quaesiveris extra* (I.7). Here in the fourth Satire Socrates uses physical imagery to emphasize that Alcibiades' knowledge
is perverted (*crura,* 42, *ilia,* 43, *nervos,* 45, *palles,* 47, *penem,* 48,
aures, 50, *respue,* 51), and he translates the injunction *nec te quaesiveris extra* into an image of a man living alone instead of with
someone else as his lover: *tecum habita: noris quam sit tibi curta
supellex* (live with yourself and you will realize how meagre your
furnishings are, 52).

Complementing this dominant metaphor of the politician as a
male prostitute are a number of interesting verbal repetitions and
contrasts. Repetition underscores the need for self-knowledge (*calles,*
5, *scis,* 10, *sapiat,* 21, *nosti,* 25, *ignotus,* 34, *novimus,* 43, *noris,* 52)
and effectively relates the opening and closing lines of the poem
through deliberate echoes (*loquere,* 8, *da verba,* 45, *potis es,* 13, *si
potes,* 46, *tollit,* 2, *tollat,* 51, and *nequiquam,* 14, 50). Similarly, the
iteration of *sorbitio* (2), *sorbere* (16), and *sorbet* (32), *despuat* (35)
and *respue* (51), *pannucia* (21) and *pannosam* (32), in Reckford's
words, "reminds the reader to look for inner connections between
these scenes." [35] Verbal contrast, on the other hand, equates Alcibiades' concern for his own skin (*summa pelle,* 14) with his high-
est spiritual goal (*summa boni,* 17) and hints that although he can
condemn others with a black mark (*nigrum theta,* 13), he cannot see
his own faults (*sum candidus,* 20).

---

[33] *Cognoscere* is the more common verb, as in Ovid, *Her.,* VI.133; cf. Colu-
mella, VI.37.9, and Tacitus, *Hist.,* IV.44. It is interesting to note, however, that
Plautus twice puns upon the double meaning of *noscere* in *Most.,* 893–894 and
Pers., 131.

[34] Némethy (ed. 1903), p. 230.

[35] Reckford, p. 487.

CHAPTER FIVE

SATIRE V

Persius' fifth Satire is justly considered his best poem. Carefully thought out both poetically and rhetorically, it represents Persius' most successful effort at reconciling the Stoic diatribe with the more informal satiric *sermo*. This Satire also contains the only lengthy passage of self-revelation in Persius' work.[1] Not surprisingly, therefore, several recent critics have discussed this Satire and Anderson, in particular, has thoroughly analyzed the imagery and verbal repetitions which unify the poem.[2] In my treatment of these devices I am deeply indebted to his analysis.

Persius does not assume the persona of an invented character in the opening lines of this Satire because he wishes to present his own experience as an argument in favor of the study of philosophy. Nevertheless he does adopt a persona inasmuch as he attempts to persuade us that he is a completely sincere person and an authority on Stoicism. The first of these qualities, his sincerity, contrasts with the insincerity of contemporary poets who, preferring myths to philosophic truths, merely repeat the well-worn clichés and formulas: *Vatibus hic mos est, centum sibi poscere voces, / centum ora et linguas optare in carmina centum* (This is the custom of bards, to ask for a hundred voices, to pray for a hundred mouths and a

---

[1] The significance of these lines describing Persius' relationship with Cornutus (30–51) has often been misunderstood. They are important not so much for the biographical information which they impart (none of it particularly unusual), but because they translate into metaphorical terms Persius' progression from potential slavery to true moral freedom. Thus they illustrate how the satirist molds autobiographical detail to his rhetorical purpose.

[2] Anderson (1960b), Wimmel, pp. 312–316, Witke (1961), pp. 66–95, and Reckford, pp. 487–494 *passim*.

hundred tongues, in their songs, 1-2).[3] The recurring images of food and hot air in these opening lines characterize their epic verse as insubstantial, a mere "banquet of tasty phrases." [4] In contrast, Cornutus points out that Persius treats the problems of everyday life (*mores,* 15, *culpam,* 16, *plebia prandia,* 18), that he knows his subject matter (*doctus,* 16), and that he uses plain language (*verba togae,* 14). The commentaries on these opening lines often assume that Persius begins to imitate the epic poets only to be restrained by Cornutus who outlines the true standards he should follow. Yet it is significant, I think, that Cornutus uses the indicative rather than the imperative (*premis,* 11, *intendis,* 13, *sequeris,* 14), thereby implying that Persius' verse already meets his standards. By attributing this praise of himself to a respected speaker like Cornutus, Persius avoids the charge of vanity while at the same time indirectly establishing his own reputation for veracity.[5] He confirms Cornutus' remarks with a promise to avoid trifles (*nugis,* 19), and instead reveal his deepest feelings. Words such as *excutienda damus praecordia* (22), *ostendisse* (24), *solidum* vs. *tectoria* (25), *voce pura,* and *totum* (28), as well as the suggestion to the reader that he is overhearing a private (and therefore probably candid) conversation, all substantiate Persius' claim to sincerity.

To present himself as an authority on Stoicism, Persius then recalls his Stoic training under Cornutus. He proves that he is qualified to speak on the theme of this Satire, the nature of moral freedom, by showing how he himself acquired this freedom.[6] During his adolescence, when he was free of parental control but at the same time most prone to give in to his passions, he submitted temporarily to Cornutus who tamed his spirit and made it obedient to reason. In this way he exchanged license for true freedom, here equated with complete unity between himself and Cornutus. Although he uses himself as an example to the reader, Persius again avoids the appear-

---

[3] Pierre Courcelle, "Histoire du cliché virgilien des cents bouches," *Rev. étud. lat.* 33 (1955): pp. 231–240, traces the long history of this commonplace from classical times through the Middle Ages.

[4] Anderson (1960b), p. 71.

[5] I do not agree with Witke (1961), pp. 66–67, that Cornutus is not the speaker in these lines. Witke argues that (1) Cornutus does not speak elsewhere in the poem, (2) if he did speak these lines the final denunciation of philosophy would be uncomplimentary to him, and (3) the vulgar idiom and convoluted syntax of these lines contradict his remarks on the need for simplicity of style. None of these arguments seems particularly convincing to me.

[6] Anderson (1960b), pp. 67, 72–73.

ance of self-righteousness by addressing his comments to Cornutus rather than to the audience.

When he turns from his own experience to a general sermon on freedom (52–191), Persius draws the reader into the poem gradually before attacking him directly in line 100. As in Satire IV, he begins with an impersonal statement: *mille hominum species et rerum discolor usus; / velle suum cuique est nec voto vivitur uno* (There are a thousand different types of men, and as many variegated ways to live; each man lives as he wishes and will not be bound by a single creed, 52–53). The subsequent illustrations of this statement are equally impersonal. Not until line 64 does Persius address his audience directly, and even then he refrains from singling out the individual reader: *petite hinc, puerique senesque, / finem animo certum miserisque viatica canis* (Seek from this philosophy, young men and old, a fixed end for your desires and provisions for your feeble grey old age, 64–65). To further mitigate his criticism Persius includes himself in the indictment (*consumpsimus,* 68), and only in line 70 does he finally turn to the reader with the familiar *te.*

Once he has introduced the reader into the poem, Persius might be expected to continue criticizing him directly, but instead he first maneuvers him, before he realizes it, into the role of the imaginary adversary. Close examination of the text reveals how skillfully Persius accomplishes this:

> libertate opus est. non hac, ut quisque Velina
> Publius emeruit, scabiosum tesserula far
> possidet. heu steriles veri, quibus una
>   Quiritem   75
> vertigo facit! hic Dama est non tresis
>   agaso,
> vappa lippus et in tenui farragine mendax.
> verterit hunc dominus, momento turbinis
>   exit
> Marcus Dama. papae! Marco spondente recusas
> credere tu nummos? Marco sub iudice palles?   80
> Marcus dixit, ita est. adsigna, Marce,
>   tabellas.
> haec mera libertas, hoc nobis pillea donant.
> "an quisquam est alius liber, nisi ducere
>   vitam
> cui licet ut libuit? licet ut volo vivere,
>   non sum
> liberior Bruto?" "mendose colligis" inquit   85
> Stoicus hic aurem mordaci lotus aceto,

"hoc relicum accipio, 'licet' illud et
    'ut volo' tolle."
"vindicta postquam meus a praetore recessi,
cur mihi non liceat, iussit quodcumque
        voluntas,
excepto siquid Masuri rubrica vetabit?"   90
disce, sed ira cadat naso rugosaque sanna,
dum veteres avias tibi de pulmone revello.

We need real freedom, not the freedom, earned by any Publius when he
joins the Veline tribe, to exchange his meal ticket for a bit of bug-ridden
grain. Alas, how barren you are of the truth, you who think that one
brief spin by his master makes a slave a free citizen. Here is Dama, not
worth a cent, bleary-eyed, and quick to lie over trifles—his master turns
him about and he comes out Marcus Dama. What? You refuse to loan
money over Marcus' signature? You grow pale when Marcus is judge?
Marcus speaks and it is so; Marcus, sign these documents. This is real lib-
erty, won when we don the cap of freedom. "But who is free except the
man who can live his life as he pleases; I can live as I wish, am I not freer
than Brutus?" "Your argument is faulty," says the Stoic, who has washed
his ears in cleansing vinegar, "I'll accept the rest if you retract 'can' and
'as I wish.'" "But after I have walked away from the praetor's rod, why
can't I do whatever I want, except what the law forbids?" Learn why,
but first wipe that angry sneer from your face while I pluck out these old
wives' tales from your breast.

Up to line 83 Persius carefully distinguishes between the reader and
Marcus Dama. Although he might equally well have used the reader
to illustrate false freedom, Persius introduces Dama instead and
throws the reader off his guard in lines 79–81 by assuming that the
latter shares his distrust of Dama. In lines 83–85, however,
the distinction between Dama and the reader fades. Dama appears to be the speaker in these lines but when the Stoic replies
he repeats the *tu* form used earlier by Persius to address the
reader. The reader is thus encouraged to identify himself with
the speaker in lines 83–85, Marcus Dama. Soon after in line 91
Persius takes over the role of the Stoic speaker, continuing to criticize the reader with the familiar *tu*.[7] Through this subtle transition,
what began as an illustration to the reader of false freedom, using
Dama and an anonymous Stoic, has become a conversation between
Persius and the reader, now identified as a freedman.

The sermon comprising the rest of the poem begins with another
series of general statements distinguishing legal and moral freedom;
soon, however, Persius turns to the reader (100) and thereafter uses

---

[7] Villeneuve (1918a), p. 334, thinks that Persius re-enters the Satire at this
point but Reckford is perhaps closer to the truth when he suggests, p. 492,
that the personalities of the two speakers merge.

him as an example of the morally enslaved man. In the other Satires the adversaries all appear to be freeborn, and often aristocratic, and it is frequently assumed that the majority of the Roman reading public belonged to this class. But in the first century A.D. the wealthy freedmen who were beginning to infiltrate the social and political domains of the old aristocratic families were anxious to acquire at least a veneer of culture and they took a great interest in literary matters. Undoubtedly they read Persius' Satires, and so it is not surprising to find Persius identifying his adversary as a freedman, as he clearly does in lines 126–131 where he hints at the adversary's recent slave status. Furthermore, like the archetypal freedman of the first century, Trimalchio, who originally amassed a fortune in commerce, the adversary makes his living in maritime trade (134–136), tries to win favor by lavish expenditures on food (177–179), and superstitiously honors all foreign cults (180–188). Persius mitigates his contempt for this man's failure to live rationally (100–108) only by a single deferential *nostrae* (115) and by the insertion of a scene from Terence's *Eunuch* (161–174), which temporarily diverts the attack to Chaerestratus. He deliberately ends his sermon on a light note, however:

> dixeris haec inter varicosos centuriones,
> continuo crassum ridet Pulfenius ingens
> et centum Graecos curto centusse licetur [189–191].

If you preached these ideas to the swollen muscled soldiers, huge Pulfenius would give a fat laugh and bid only a clipped hundred piece for a hundred Greeks.

These lines do more than counteract Persius' previous harshness, for although he has just proved conclusively that the reader is as ignorant as Pulfenius, Persius here overlooks his previous remarks and bids for the reader's goodwill by identifying him with the philosopher (*dixeris*).

In his discussion of the imagery of this Satire, W. S. Anderson argues that Persius' obscurity arises, paradoxically, from his attempt to clarify his ideas through "an accumulation of metaphors." In his words, "Persius' effort for precision of phrase forces him to compensate with a series of explanatory comments that plunge him into thematic imprecision." [8] Answering the judgment of most critics that no logical connection exists between Persius' conversation with Cornutus (1–51) and his diatribe on freedom (73–191), Anderson demonstrates that the connection is a poetic one reinforced through

---

[8] Anderson (1960b), p. 66.

parallel images and verbal repetition. The numerous allusions to food in the second half of the Satire, for example, correspond to the descriptions of epic poetry as food in the first half. Together they suggest that the epic poet and the freedman are equally enslaved: "The true slave fails to discern the essential values of life when he makes money or superstition the criterion according to which he will eat. Equally servile, the grand poet ignores the significance of his subject, debasing epic or tragedy to a banquet of tasty phrases." [9] A second series of images emphasizes the lack of control common to the poet and the slave. The poet has so little command of his material that he needs a hundred mouths to recite it (1–2), he bursts his cheeks declaiming (*rumpere*, 13), and he spews forth hot air like a bellows (*coquitur*, 10, *premis*, 11). In the second half of the poem these same words denote the freedman's lack of self-control (*decoquit*, 57, *presso*, 109, *rupi*, 158).

Both as a poet and a Stoic Persius contrasts with these two slavish figures. His style is sharp and precise (*acri*, 14, *radere*, 15, *defigere*, 16), his phrases are moderate (*ore modico*, 15) and, significantly, his vocabulary and wit are characteristic of a freeborn Roman (*verba togae*, 14, *ingenuo ludo*, 16).[10] Furthermore, having learned true freedom through his Stoic training, Persius enjoys complete unity of purpose with Cornutus, while the passions of other men pull them in different directions. As Anderson notes, the dominant metaphor here is expressed in terms of number. Before he met Cornutus Persius was faced with multiple courses of action (*iter ambiguum*, 34, *ramosa compita*, 35), but now he and Cornutus live in complete harmony (*unum*, 43, 46, 50, *disponimus ambo*, 43, *foedere certo*, 45, *consentire*, 46, *concordia fata*, 49). Other men, however, differ in their goals (*mille species, discolor usus*, 52), and serve many masters (*tot rebus*, 124, *duplici, diversum*, 154, *ancipiti*, 156). In connection with this number imagery Anderson remarks upon the references to *centum* (1, 2, 6, 191) and the punning use of this word in *centuriones* (189), and *centusse* (191). These repetitions effectively emphasize the slavish condition of the contemporary epic poets and those who join Pulfenius in scoffing at philosophy.

---

[9] *Ibid.*, p. 71. Most of the verbal repetitions which I have summarized in the following paragraphs are discussed at greater length by Anderson, pp. 71–75.

[10] *Ibid.*, pp. 71–72. The adjective *teres* (15) also suggests the Stoic idea of moral freedom since it recalls Horace's description of the truly free man as one *in se ipso totus, teres, atque rotundus* (totally self-sufficient, round and smooth, *Ser.*, II.7.86).

Anderson also points out several other verbal repetitions which distinguish Cornutus and Persius from the rest of society. Whereas Persius follows the speech of free men (*verba togae sequeris*, 14), most men slavishly follow their desires (*sectabere*, 71, *sequeris*, 155, *obsequio*, 156), and do not know the proper goals to pursue (*sequenda*, 107). Persius also denies that he is interested in trifles (*nugis*, 19); later this word describes the slavish mentality (*nugator*, 127, *nugaris*, 169). Cornutus, too, is contrasted with the slave by the repetition of *dulcis amice* (23), *dulcis amicis* (109), *dinoscere* (24, 105), and *in pectore fixi* (27), *in pectore* (117), and *sub pectore* (144). But perhaps the most complex expression of this contrast occurs in Persius' assertion that he and Cornutus share the same horoscope, *Saturnumque gravem nostro Iove frangimus una* (Together we have broken heavy Saturn with Jove, 50). This line, Anderson argues, invokes the traditional association of Saturn with license and Juppiter with order and reason. In saying that he and Cornutus have "broken heavy Saturn with Jove," Persius in effect summarizes the significance of his Stoic education: with Cornutus' help he learned to substitute reason for license, thus acquiring true freedom. The verb *frangimus*, suggesting an image of liberating oneself from fetters, emphasizes the difference between Persius and the rest of men who are slaves to their irrational passions.[11]

In addition to the verbal correspondences noted by Anderson, there are several others which strengthen the contrast between Persius and other men.[12] The verb *ducere*, for example, appears first in a poetic context (4), then occurs several times in philosophic passages. When his ignorance threatened to lead Persius astray (*diducit*, 35), Cornutus took control and molded his character (*ducit*, 40); hence his life and Cornutus' are guided by the same horoscope (*duci*, 46). In contrast, the adversary later falsely equates freedom with the ability to lead life as one wishes (*ducere vitam*, 83), and Persius twice uses this same verb to connote moral enslavement (118, 176). The repetition of *ducere* complements the reiteration of *sequi* noted earlier. Similarly, Persius is able to heal *pallentis mores* (15), and Cornutus grows pale studying philosophy (62), while other men seek the pale cumin in trade (55) or blanch with fear (80, 184). The Fate of Persius and Cornutus, moreover, is *tenax veri* (48), whereas other men deceive or are victims of deceit (77,

---

[11] Anderson, pp. 76–80.

[12] Undoubtedly Anderson recognized these additional repetitions, but was unable, through limitations of space, to include them in his article.

85, 106). Persius also describes the Stoic *regula* as *sollers* (37), and later, in contrast, applies this same epithet to the Epicurean *Luxuria* (142).

A number of single repetitions reveal lesser connections in the poem. Persius and Cornutus spend their days in fruitful study while other men procrastinate (*consumere*, 41, cf. 68); Persius talks to Cornutus in private (*secrete*, 21), just as Reason later whispers good advice (*secretam*, 96); and Persius' reference to the adversary's skill at discerning truth (*calles*, 105) echoes Cornutus' earlier praise of Persius (*iunctura callidus acri*, 14). The adversary in the scene with *Avaritia* and *Luxuria* is also related through verbal repetition to other servile figures in the poem (*recens piper*, 136, cf. 54–55, *pellem*, 140, cf. 116, *aptas*, 140, cf. 95, *indulge*, 151, cf. 57, *dulcia*, 151, cf. 109 vs. 23). And, finally, in the description of the superstitious fears provoked by foreign religions there are a number of repetitions relating these lines to the opening lines of the poem (*nebulam*, 181, cf. 7, *tumet*, 183, cf. 13, *grandes*, 186, cf. 7, *incussere*, *inflantis*, 187, cf. *anhelanti*, 10, *ventos*, 11, *caput*, 188, cf. 18).[13]

In this Satire Persius appears to have acquired complete poetic control of the techniques with which he was experimenting in earlier poems. Every detail, each image and verbal repetition, contributes to the thematic and artistic unity of the whole, yet, most remarkably, none of these connections are so obvious as to intrude upon the informal conversational façade of the Satire. Indeed it would not be an understatement to say that this Satire eloquently illustrates Longinus' maxim that "art is only perfect when it looks like nature, and nature succeeds only by concealing art about her person."[14]

SATIRE VI

Satire VI is quite different from Persius' other poems. While the latter resemble the Stoic sermon in varying degrees, this Satire has

---

[13] Other significant repetitions include *turgescat* (20, cf. 56), *laxamus* (44, 110, 125), *crepet* (25, 127), *dulcis* (23, 109, 151), *frangimus* (50, 165), *trahe* (17, 28, 160) *fronte* (104, 116), and *acri* (14, 127). Note, too, Persius' emphasis upon the failure of external apparel (*purpura*, 30, *bulla*, 31, *umbo*, 33) to provide the proper protection for *intortos mores* (38).

[14] Longinus, *On the Sublime*, XX.1, tr. by W. Hamilton Fyfe (Cambridge, 1960), p. 193.

all the characteristics of an Horatian epistle: the introductory lines addressed to a close friend inquiring where he is and what he is doing, the conversational tone, the abrupt shifts in subject matter and informal organization favored by Horace, and the philosophic advice, "enjoy, enjoy" (*utar ego, utar,* 22), which seems oddly inconsistent with the traditional picture of Persius as a sober, serious person. Reckford has drawn attention to the Horatian quality of this Satire, particularly its similarity to *Epistle,* II.2, but no critic to my knowledge has yet recognized the extent of this similarity.[15] For his subject matter, imagery, and tone Persius is greatly indebted to Horace's epistle; but he does not imitate this poem as closely as he imitated the *Alcibiades I* in Satire IV. Instead he adapts certain Horatian elements to his own purposes. A comparison of the two works will clarify this point.

In *Epistle,* II.2, written a few years after the publication of *Odes* I–III (23 B.C.), Horace defends his decision to give up lyric poetry in favor of philosophy.[16] His friend Florus wrote requesting some lyrics (*carmina,* 25) and in reply Horace explains why he cannot oblige. Now in his mid-forties, he no longer feels a close kinship with the subjects of lyric verse: *singula de nobis anni praedantur euntes; / eripuere iocos, Venerem, convivia, ludum* (The passing years rob us of pleasures one by one, snatching away laughter and love, banquets and games, 55–56). Then, too, everyone has different tastes and he cannot please them all (58–64). There are also too many distractions in the city, *tot curas totque labores* (66). Later on Horace twice reverts to this theme, once when he says enviously,

> scriptorum chorus omnis amat nemus et
> fugit urbem,
> rite cliens Bacchi somno gaudentis et
> umbra,
> tu me inter strepitus nocturnos atque
> diurnos
> vis canere et contracta sequi vestigia
> vatum? [77–80].

The entire chorus of writers loves the woodlands and flees the city, faithful clients of Bacchus who revels in sleep and shade. Do you expect me, hemmed in night and day by the city's roar, to write and follow the poets' narrow path?

---

[15] Reckford, p. 497.

[16] This poem is generally dated *ca.* 23–17 B.C. Brink, p. 184, n. 1, argues that it was composed after *Epistles* I (20 B.C.) between 19 and 18 B.C. Horace kept to his decision until 17 B.C. when he composed the *Carmen Saeculare.* Recent discussions of this epistle include Brink, pp. 183–190 and M. J. McGann, "Horace's Epistle to Florus (Epist. 2.2)," *Rhein. Mus.* 97 (1954): pp. 343–358.

and again when—significantly for Persius' Satire—he compares the
city to a tempest-torn sea:

> . . . hic ego rerum
> fluctibus in mediis et tempestatibus
>   urbis
> verba lyrae motura sonum conectere
>   digner? [84–86][17]

Caught in the tide of events, in a storm-tossed city, am I fit to join together words to wake the voice of the lyre?

Horace also dislikes the mutual back-scratching which he must endure among his colleagues (87–105). Finally, he says that he would
rather write with less care and preserve his peace of mind than
worry constantly about maintaining the high standards required of
a good poet (126–128). Here, of course, he speaks with ultimate
irony since it is his ability to maintain these high standards which
makes him a superior poet.[18] Nevertheless, he is completely serious
when he enunciates the artistic criteria of the poet *qui legitimum
cupiet fecisse poema* (who wishes to write a true poem, 109). The
good poet, he says, must criticize his own style severely, removing
undignified words and reviving forgotten ones:

> obscurata diu populo bonus eruet atque
> proferet in lucem speciosa vocabula rerum,
> quae priscis memorata Catonibus atque
>   Cethegis
> nunc situs informis premit et deserta
>   vetustas [115–118].

The good poet will dust off and bring to light for people fine words long
forgotten, words once made memorable by Cato and Cethegus and now
bowed down by crude neglect and lonely old age.

He need not avoid new words, but he must consistently strive for
a smooth, forceful style and, most important, appear to achieve it
effortlessly (109–125).

Horace then turns in the second half of the poem to a more
serious reason for abandoning lyric verse:

> nimirum sapere est abiectis utile nugis,
> et tempestivum pueris concedere ludum,
> ac non verba sequi fidibus modulanda
>   Latinis,
> sed verae numerosque modosque ediscere vitae [141–144].

Doubtless it's time to put aside trifles for wisdom, yield the playful pastimes
suited to youth, and no longer pursue words measured to the Latin lyre,
but learn instead the rhythms and meters of life.

---

[17] In Satire VI the sea symbolizes danger and discomfort; cf. *infra,* p. 88.
[18] McGann, p. 356.

The rest of the epistle, illustrating the kind of subject matter which Horace intends to treat, discusses the proper use of riches and appears to have influenced Persius' Satire most directly. Horace defines possession by use rather than by ownership through financial transaction; since no one owns anything permanently but merely uses it during his brief stay on earth, the accumulation of wealth is pointless and one might as well enjoy it while one can (146–179). The proper attitude toward wealth is neither that of the excessively frugal man nor the prodigal, here represented by two brothers, but somewhere in between where Horace places himself:

> utar et ex modico quantum res poscet acervo
> tollam, nec metuam quid de me iudicet heres,
> quod non plura datis invenerit: et tamen idem
> scire volam, quantum simplex hilarisque nepoti
> discrepet et quantum discordet parcus avaro [190–194].

May I spend my wealth and take whatever I need from my small pile without worrying what my heir will think when he finds the little I've left him. At the same time I hope I have the ear to distinguish the difference between the simple, happy spender and the prodigal, the thrifty man and the miser.

A few lines later Horace repeats the sea image used earlier, this time comparing life to a voyage (199–202). He then warns against other vices equally as dangerous as avarice and closes with an image familiar from Lucretius:

> lusisti satis, edisti satis atque bibisti:
> tempus abire tibi est, ne potum largius
>   aequo
> rideat et pulset lasciva decentius aetas [214–216].[19]

You have played enough, dined and drunk your fill; it is time for you to leave before youth jeers you, in your cups, with fitting wantonness.

As I remarked earlier, Persius appears at first to have ignored Horace's preliminary remarks on poetry and imitated only his sermon on riches. From Horace's statement that he will enjoy himself and disregard his heir's complaints, Persius derives the theme of most of his Satire (33–74). He also applies Horace's definition of the happy man as one *posset qui ignoscere servis / et signo laeso non insanire lagoenae* (who can forgive his servants and not lose his mind over the broken seal of a pilfered wine bottle, 133–134) to himself when he says that he does not wish *cenare sine uncto / et signum in vapida naso tetigisse lagoena* (to dine without a little olive oil, and to sniff the cork when the wine is served flat, 16–17).

[19] Cf. Lucretius, III.938–939. Horace also alludes in these closing lines to his decision to give up lyric poetry (cf. *ludum*, 56, 142, *lusisti*, 214).

Furthermore, Horace's example of the two brothers, one frugal and one prodigal, reappears in Persius' Satire accompanied by a similar reference to their *varo genio* (18–19, cf. *Epis.*, II.2.187, *Genius*). And, finally, Persius, like Horace, stresses the importance of land as a source of wealth.

The influence of Horace's epistle upon the sixth Satire is not confined, however, to these obvious verbal echoes from the sermon on riches. In a different way the first half of Persius' poem also owes a great deal to Horace, for in these lines Persius describes his friend Caesius Bassus, to whom the poem is addressed, in terms strongly reminiscent of Horace's portrait of the ideal lyric poet. Bassus was a writer whose lyric poetry earned him a place along with Horace in Quintilian's list of recommended authors (X.1.96), and although he was undoubtedly influenced to some extent by Horace, Persius, I think, goes further in these lines and deliberately portrays him as Horace's successor.

In defending his decision to give up lyric poetry, Horace implies that this verse is insubstantial, intended primarily to amuse, and more suitable for a young man than for an older person. He also points out that the poet needs a quiet atmosphere such as the country offers, and in defining the duties of a conscientious poet he mentions that of reviving old and forgotten words. Persius' lines to Bassus allude to all of these themes. Bassus has retreated to the country in winter and is writing lyrics (*lyra,* 2); but these poems are not merely trifles because although they amuse (*agitare iocos,* 5), they also contain a moralizing element here suggested by the adjectives *honesto* (5) and *egregius* (6). In addition Bassus disproves Horace, for despite his advanced age (*senex,* 6), he still appeals to a youthful audience (*iuvenes,* 5). Bassus also fulfills Horace's requirements for the good poet because he has revived earlier Latin words in verse: *mire opifex numeris veterum primordia vocum / atque marem strepitum fidis intendisse Latinae* (You have skillfully fitted the origins of ancient words and the manly sound of the Latin harp to the rhythms of verse, 3–4). The phrase *veterum primordia vocum,* consciously echoing Lucretius' description of the first sounds as *primordia vocum* (IV.531), suggested to Villeneuve that Persius here refers to a poem by Bassus on the etymology of old words.[20] This is quite possible since Bassus is believed to be the

---

[20] Villeneuve (1918b), p. 160, after mentioning this interpretation, rejects it, preferring to see in the phrase *veterum primordia vocum* an allusion to the meters of the early Greek lyric poets. But since C. Bailey, ed., *Titi Lucreti*

author of a treatise on metrics mentioned by several later grammarians and he seems to have been a scholar as well as a poet.[21]
The phrase *fidis Latinae,* undoubtedly inspired by Horace's *fidibus
Latinis (Epis.,* II.2.143), further emphasizes Bassus' interest in the
native Roman poetic tradition. On the basis of these parallels between the two poems, I suggest that Persius wrote these lines in
reply to Horace, and that they are not simply "a device of the poet
to reach the point of telling us where he is." [22]

In his other Satires Persius assumes the roles of the rebellious
poet, the Stoic philosopher, Socrates, and the grateful protégé of
Cornutus. Here he speaks in his own person but he most resembles
Horace, the advocate of moderate enjoyment. He shares Horace's
disdain for the crowd *(securus volgi,* 12) and when he says that he
has no interest in increasing his property, *securus et angulus ille /
vicini nostro quia pinguior* (not even caring that the adjoining corner of my neighbor's field is more fertile than mine, 13–14), he consciously echoes Horace's illustration of what he does *not* pray for:
o si angulus ille / proximus accedat qui nunc denormat agellum!
(if only I could acquire that nearby corner which now distorts the
shape of my little field, *Ser.,* II.6.8–9). Persius also qualifies his philosophy of indulgence, as Horace does, with a warning against going to extremes:

> . . . utar ego, utar,
> nec rhombos ideo libertis ponere lautus
> nec tenuis sollers turdarum nosse salivas [22–24].[23]

May I spend what I have and spend some more, yet not be gauche enough
to serve my freedmen trout, nor gourmet enough to distinguish the sex
of a thrush by its taste.

Cari de rerum natura libri sex (repr., Oxford, 1950) 1: p. 389, translates *primordia
vocum* as "the first-beginnings of voices," and explains, *ibid.,* 3: p. 1244, that
they are not atoms but "particles which issue from the lungs," it is difficult to
see how the phrase can refer to Greek meters. *Vox, voces* is often used in a
transferred sense to mean "words"; cf. Cicero, *Mur.,* XXV.50, Caesar, *Bell.
Gall.,* I.39, Horace, *Odes,* IV.6.22, Quintilian, V.7.36.

[21] References to Bassus' treatise can be found in H. Keil, *Grammatici Latini*
(Leipzig, 1857–1880) 1: 513.15, 2: 527.16, 6: 209, 10: 395. line 2358 and 396.
line 2369, and 555.22. Most of these references speak highly of him as the
author of a treatise on the iambic meter dedicated to Nero. This work may
be identical with the treatise entitled *De metris* and attributed erroneously
to Atilius Fortunatianus; cf. Keil, 6: pp. 255–272. Keil also includes a spurious
work assigned to Bassus, 1: pp. 305–312.

[22] Villeneuve (1918a), p. 338.

[23] Cf. Villeneuve (1918b), p. 166. I do not agree with him, however, that
these lines are both examples of prodigality. The lines from Horace (192–194),
quoted on p. 81, imply that a contrast is intended.

These few details, unfortunately, do not create a vivid character, and one might justly argue that it is very difficult, if not impossible, for a satirist to portray a historic person. Stock fictional figures such as the angry young poet in Satire I or the Stoic philosopher in Satires II and III are easier roles because they are types rather than individuals with historically documented character traits. The persona of Socrates in Satire IV offers a possible solution to the problem; there Persius does not attempt to recreate the historic Socrates but instead reproduces his manner of argument. His task is somewhat easier because Socrates as a philosopher was known primarily through his fictional role in the Platonic dialogues. Here in Satire VI, I think, Persius tries in a similar way to reproduce Horace's persona by echoing several of his statements in a light, ironic tone. He manages to sound like Horace but the latter's persona is too painstakingly developed, with a wealth of minute detail, to be recreated in a single poem. Nor does Persius individualize the other characters in this Satire. He involves the audience only briefly in line 25, when he turns unobtrusively from talking to Bassus and addresses someone with whom the reader identifies. This speaker, I believe, interrupts in line 33 to protest that his heir will object if he gives away his property; soon thereafter he is replaced in the role of adversary by Persius' hypothetical heir. This heir is an equally anonymous figure, however, whose only personality trait is his greed. These speakers resemble both the shadowy figures who appear here and there in Horace's first book of *Sermones,* and the adversary in Persius' second Satire. The latter poem, I believe, is an early work and, since the imagery patterns in Satire VI are developed in a manner similar to those in Satire II, through a series of contrasted abstractions, I suggest Satire VI is also an early work, perhaps Persius' first effort at satire. It would not be unusual for Persius to begin his career by imitating Horace, since classical theory advocated the imitation of earlier models, and then gradually to develop his own originality.

To my knowledge only one critic, Reckford, has commented upon the imagery of this Satire. He says:

Too, Satire 6 differs in imagery from the others. There is no latent disease, no perversion, no strong contrast between appearance and reality. Instead there is a dominant metaphor of land and sea: the sea may cause shipwreck, like misfortune [*sic*]; if it 'winters', one may retreat to a warm shore (compare Lucretius' shores of light, an image of life). Land supplies all good things; one should draw upon it to the utmost, free to use capital as well as income. . . . Our ties to the land make us all 'sons of earth'; we must submit to the kinship of humanity. Taken together, land and sea are metaphors of the human condition, Persius' deductions from which are thoroughly un-Stoic.[24]

Reckford recognizes the important contrast in this poem between land and sea but he does not mention two additional contrasts, those of country life vs. city life, and Roman *mores* vs. Greek customs. All three themes are interrelated: mastery of the sea leads to the rise of cities and commerce and, eventually, to the introduction of foreign goods and customs which displace the old values and simple country ways. Persius does not develop these contrasts with the careful organization evident in the third or fifth Satire, but instead suggests their presence and possible interrelationship through recurrent patterns of imagery.

As he does again in the second and fifth Satires, Persius establishes the positive values in the opening lines of the poem:

> Admovit iam bruma foco te, Basse, Sabino?
> iamne lyra et tetrico vivunt tibi pectine
>   chordae?
> mire opifex numeris veterum primordia vocum
> atque marem strepitum fidis intendisse
>   Latinae,
> mox iuvenes agitare iocos et pollice honesto
> egregius lusisse senex [1–6].

Has winter already driven you, Bassus, to your Sabine hearth? Do the lyre's strings now come to life at the sharp stroke of your thumb? You have skillfully fitted the origins of ancient words and the manly sound of the Latin harp to the rhythms of verse; now, adept as ever in middle age, you will soon provoke youthful pleasure and give delight with a worthy song.

In these lines Persius develops Horace's brief image of the lyre of life (*Epis.*, II.2.144) into a metaphor contrasting Greek and Roman values. The references to *Sabino, tetrico,* and *marem strepitum . . . fidis Latinae* evoke an image of the simple, austere life of early Rome, full of strength and virility.[25] This image, connected with the old Latin term for lyre, *fidis,* implicitly opposes the more effete Greek way of life suggested by the newer Greek loanword, *lyra.*[26] These opening lines also associate the Roman countryside

---

[24] Reckford, pp. 497–498.

[25] As the name of a mountain in Sabine territory, *tetrico* is practically a synonym for *Sabino;* cf. Ovid, *Amores,* III.8.61, Vergil, *Aen.,* VII.713, Livy, I.18.

[26] *Fidis* occurs in Plautus, *Epid.,* 473, 500, 514, Terence, *Eun.,* 133, Varro, frg. Nonius (ed. Lindsay, p. 212), and Cicero, *de Or.,* III.216, *De fin.,* IV.75, and *De rep.,* II.69, among others. Plautus uses *lyra* once in a Greek quote and Cicero also uses it once. It does not become common until the late first

with warmth and withdrawal, suggesting security. Bassus is warmed by his Sabine hearth which visually encloses him, while the Ligurian coast grows warm for Persius (*intepet,* 7) and retreats into many sheltered inlets (*receptat,* 8). Persius further emphasizes the idea of retreat by describing himself as *securus volgi* (12) and by calling Bassus *egregius* with a hint of its root meaning, "outside the crowd." [27]

After he has established these positive values with the Roman countryside, Persius introduces a verse of Ennius:

> "Lunai portum, est operae, cognoscite, cives."
> cor iubet hoc Enni, postquam destertuit esse
> Maeonides Quintus pavone ex Pythagoreo [9–11].

"Recognize the harbor of Luna, citizens." Ennius' heart gave this command after he stopped snoring and dreaming that he had turned into Quintus, the son of Homer, from a Pythagorean peacock.

According to the scholiast, line 9 occurs in the beginning of the *Annales* which recounts Ennius' famous dream when Homer appeared and announced that his soul had passed into a peacock and thence into Ennius' body.[28] In his edition of Ennius, Vahlen offers the attractive suggestion that Ennius draws attention to Luna in this line because the dream occurred there.[29] But why does Persius

---

century B.C. when it appears frequently in Horace and the elegists. The distinction between *fidis* and *lyra,* as well as the difference of tenses in these opening lines, suggest to me that perhaps Persius alludes here to two different works by Bassus, a poem on Latin etymologies which he has already completed (*intendisse*) and a series of lyrics in Greek meters which he is now working on (*vivunt, agitare*). Although *mox* in this period often means "soon afterward," Persius may be using it here in its original sense of "soon," implying future publication. It is true, of course, that he substitutes *lusisse* for the expected *ludere,* but this substitution may be due to metrical necessity or perhaps imitates the Greek aorist. Cf. E. Merone, "L'infinito aoristico in Persio," *Giornale ital. di filol.* 7 (1954): pp. 244–255, and M. Leumann, J. Hofmann, and A. Szantyr, *Lateinische Grammatik* (Munich, 1963–1965) 1: pp. 351–352.

[27] Anderson (1960a), p. 233, provides a parallel for this use of *egregius* in Horace's phrase *egregio corpore* (*Ser.,* I.6.67).

[28] Cf. the scholion on line 10:

> Hunc versum ad suum carmen de Ennii carminibus transtulit. . . . Sic enim ait Ennius in annalium suorum principio, ubi se dicit vidisse in somnis Homerum dicentem, fuisse se quondam pavonem, et ex eo translatam esse animam in se, secundum Pythagorae philosophi diffinitionem [*sic*].

He has transferred this line from Ennius' poem to his own, . . . for Ennius speaks thus in the opening of the *Annales* when he says that in a dream he saw Homer saying that he had been a peacock and then his soul had been transferred to him [Ennius], according to the doctrine of Pythagoras.

[29] I. Vahlen, ed., *Ennianae Poesis Reliquiae* (Leipzig, 1903), p. cxlix.

quote the line at this point and what is the precise meaning of lines 10–11? Is Persius merely referring to Ennius awaking from his dream or does he mean, "after Ennius ceased to write Greek-inspired poetry and turned to Roman affairs for his subject matter"? Since Persius earlier expressed a preference for the Roman way of life, the latter explanation proposed by Housman is tempting, but unfortunately there is no evidence to support it.[30] Not only is Ennius' poetry predominantly Greek in inspiration, but Persius in the prologue cites him as an example of a Latin poet who preferred the Greek tradition to the Roman.[31] Furthermore his derisive attitude toward Ennius in the prologue reappears here in the verb *destertuit* and the oxymoron *Maeonides Quintus*.[32] In lieu of Housman's interpretation the poetic context offers another explanation. Both before and after the reference to Ennius Persius mentions that he is staying on the Ligurian coast (*Ligus ora*, 6, *hic*, 12). Since the harbor of Luna (modern La Spezia) is located on this coast, it is possible that Persius is wintering there and recalls Ennius' words.[33] A few lines earlier, moreover, Persius emphasized the warmth and security of the countryside (1, 7), and in subsequent lines he reiterates this idea, contrasting it to the coldness and danger of the sea (7, 27–31). The fact therefore that he specifically refers to the harbor of Luna rather than to the town suggests to me that he is saying, in effect, "recognize the value of staying at home, safe in a snug harbor, and living off the land." [34]

The recommendation to live off the land leads naturally to the idea of the produce of land, food. The importance of food imagery in this Satire supports Anderson's contention that "a man's attitude towards food can define his character." [35] The miser denies himself the pleasure of even a little olive oil (*cenare sine uncto*, 16) and scrutinizes his wine supply minutely (17); similarly, when he

---

[30] A. E. Housman, "Ennius in Pers. VI.9," *Class. Rev.* 48 (1934): pp. 50–51.

[31] Cf. *supra*, p. 18.

[32] J. H. Waszink, "Varia critica et exegetica," *Mnemosyne* 3, 11 (1943): p. 70.

[33] The identification of Luna with La Spezia is not completely proven. L. Pareti, "Portus Lunae," *Atene e Roma* 21–22 (1918–1919): pp. 131–158, suggests that the site mentioned by Persius is the ancient city of Luni on the Macra (ancient Mastra) River in Etruria, on the border of Liguria. Cf. also the recent Swedish excavations at Luni sul Mignone in King Gustaf Adolf of Sweden and Axel Boethius, *Etruscan Culture, Land, and People* (New York, 1963), pp. 320–328.

[34] For an interpretation of *Lunai portum* as an allusion to Pythagoreanism, see E. Griset, " 'LUNAI PORTUM' o 'lunai portum'," *Riv. di stud. class.* 2 (1954): pp. 13–16.

[35] Anderson (1960), p. 71.

borrows Horace's example of the avaricious man and the prodigal,
Persius characterizes them by their attitude toward food (19–22).
As I pointed out earlier, Persius also defines his adherence to the
golden mean in terms of serving turbot and thrushes (23–24), and
later in the poem he uses the image of dousing a cabbage with oil,
albeit ironically, to symbolize the life of enjoyment (68–69). These
images as well as the numerous other references to food in this
Satire are perhaps inspired by Horace's concluding metaphor of
the banquet of life from which we take our fill and depart.[36]

These first twenty-six lines thus develop the positive side of
Persius' argument by associating several abstract concepts with the
Roman countryside: strength, virility, warmth, security, an abundance of food, and the good life. Persius now turns to the hardships
incurred by those who prefer the sea to the land and foreign imports to domestic goods. The shipwreck described in lines 27–33
occurs off the southeast coast of Italy, indicating that perhaps this
merchant was returning home from Greece or the Near East, and
the lofty tone of these lines emphasizes the magnitude of the loss.[37]
The man stores up his capital in the sea (condidit, 29), instead of
in a treasure chest,[38] and far from providing food for his family,
he himself almost becomes food for cormorants (obvia mergis, 30).
In addition the phrase surda vota (28) and the loss of the ingentes
dei (30) hint that even the gods do not approve of his ventures.
Underlining this contrast between the sea which is dangerous to
the merchant but hospitable and personal to the man on land
(meum mare, 7), are the verbal repetitions of ingens (7), ingentes
(30), scopuli (8), saxa (27), and litus (8), litore (29).

The condemnation of sea travel contains an implicit condemnation, also, of imported goods and customs. As an example Persius
chooses the spice trade and the custom of burning quantities of
spices at funerals. The adversary fears that if he donates a piece
of land to his shipwrecked friend his heir will not burn enough
spices on his pyre:

> . . . "sed cenam funeris heres
> negleget iratus quod rem curtaveris; urnae
> ossa inodora dabit, seu spirent cinnama surdum

---

[36] Additional references to food occur in lines 33, 40, 50, 69–71, and 74.
[37] Villeneuve (1918a), p. 492, remarks on the echoes of Horace, Epod.,
X.21–22 and Vergil, Aen., II.15–16 and VII.463 in these lines.
[38] Condere often carries the connotation of storing up for the future; cf.
Cicero, Clu. XXVI.72, Nat. Deor., II.63.157, Varro, Res Rust., I.62, Horace,
Epis., I.1.12 and II.1.140, Odes, I.1.9, and Martial, XIII.111.2.

seu ceraso peccent casiae nescire paratus.
tune bona incolumis minuas?" et Bestius urguet
doctores Graios: "ita fit; postquam sapere urbi
cum pipere et palmis venit nostrum hoc maris
     expers,
fenisecae crasso vitiarunt unguine pultes" [33–40].

"Your heir, in a rage, will forget your funeral banquet because you've curtailed his inheritance. He will bury your bones in an urn without any perfume and never notice that the cinnamon has lost its scent and the *casia* is mixed with cherry wood. Can you borrow from your estate and get away with it?" And Bestius taunts the learned Greeks: "That's the way it is now; ever since our home-grown wisdom (not the imported kind) came in with the pepper and dates and tasted city life, the farmers have been spoiling their porridge with thick perfume."

Villeneuve, overlooking the general patterns of imagery in this Satire, argues that generosity is the imported product which Bestius attacks.[39] Since he specifically refers to spices and unguents, however, his words *ita fit* probably refer back to the use of these items at funerals. In effect Bestius protests that foreign customs have undermined the old Roman values to such an extent that not only have spices replaced simpler funerary offerings, but now the Roman farmers even put perfume in their porridge.[40] Pliny's comments on the spice trade in the first century A.D. support this interpretation. Although the custom of burning spices, especially cinnamon and *casia,* at Roman funerals may have begun as early as the first century B.C. when Rome began to trade with the East, Pliny labels this custom a luxury and points out that

periti rerum adseverant non ferre [Arabiam] tantum annuo fetu quantum Nero princeps novissimo Poppaeae suae die concremaverit [A.D., 65 *Hist. Nat.,* XII.41.83].[41]

Experts have asserted that Arabia's entire annual crop [of spices] did not equal the amount burned by the emperor Nero at Poppaea's funeral.

Despite the vast quantity of spices burned every year at funerals, Pliny argues, the gods in olden days *nec minus propitii erant mola*

---

[39] Villeneuve (1918a), pp. 340–341.

[40] Cf. Pliny, *Hist. Nat.,* XIII.5.25, on the uses of perfumes:

at, Hercules, iam quidam etiam in potus addunt, tantique est amaritudo ut odore prodigo fruatur ex utraque parte corpus.

Men even add them to their drinks, by Hercules, and the essence is so powerful that it exudes from every pore.

[41] Cf. Tacitus, *Ann.,* XVI.6. The spice trade became so large in the late first century that Vespasian converted Nero's portico below the Palatine into a spice market, the Horrea Piperataria. For additional information on the spices traded and their prices, see Tenney Frank, *An Economic Survey of Ancient Rome* (Baltimore, 1940) 5: pp. 231, 284–286.

salsa supplicantibus, immo vero, ut palam est, placatiores (were no less favorable to suppliants offering a handful of salted grain; in fact, as is obvious, they were better satisfied, *ibid.*). The remarkable similarity between the attitudes of Pliny and Bestius indicates that even in the first century A.D. there were those who looked back with longing to the days when customs were simpler. As a conclusion to this section (27–40), Bestius' words are carefully chosen to summarize the three major contrasts of the poem. Urban influences are vitiating the old rural way of life (city vs. country), and native customs which have not traveled over the sea (*maris expers*) are being driven out by foreign ones (land vs. sea, domestic *mores* vs. foreign imports).[42]

The same point seems to be made in lines 43–52, where Persius proposes with great irony to celebrate Caligula's German victory with a hundred pairs of gladiators and public distributions of food. These projects and the triumph itself, a staged affair with rented props, are comparable to elaborate funerals (33–37): both are extravagant displays involving foreign imports and designed to impress the public. Persius' scorn for imported goods echoes in the references to *chlamydas, gausapa, esseda,* and *Rhenos* (46–47), while the verbal repetitions of *ingentes* (30, 47), *dis* (30, 48), *excutitur* (45, 75), *largior* (32, 51), *iuvenes* (5) and *pubis* (44), and *egregius* (6, cf. 49, *popello,* 50) contrast foolish investments in commerce and public *munera* with worthwhile pursuits such as aiding an indigent friend or writing poetry. Persius' heir does not vigorously protest this curtailing of his future inheritance, however, presumably because he is afraid to speak out: *an prohibes? dic clare. "non adeo" inquis / "exossatus ager iuxta est"* (Are you going to stop me? Speak up! "The field nearby," you say, "is not yet cleared of stones," 51–52). This cryptic reply admits of several interpretations, none entirely satisfactory.[43] Perhaps the simplest explanation is that proposed by the scholiast and accepted recently by Clausen.[44] The scholiast understands *adeo* as "yet" and interprets *exossatus* (lit.

---

[42] The phrase *maris expers* is an example of *amphibolia* since it means both "lacking experience of the sea" and "lacking virility." In the latter sense it describes Roman customs as they have been vitiated by foreign influences. Cf. Housman (1913), p. 28. The phrase clearly contrasts with *marem strepitum* (4).

[43] The question arises whether to take *adeo* as an adverb, "yet," or as a verb with *hereditatem* understood, meaning "I accept the inheritance." Villeneuve (1918b), p. 174, gives an extensive discussion of the problem.

[44] Cf. Clausen (1963), p. 31, who quotes the scholia.

"without bones") metaphorically to mean "not yet cleared of stones," on the basis of Deucalion's remark in the *Metamorphoses* that *lapides in corpore terrae ossa reor dici* (I think that stones are called the bones of the earth, I.393–394). Since Persius earlier had advised his heir to withdraw from the crowd (42), the scholiast understands the heir to mean that he is afraid of being stoned by the mob if he voices disapproval of games and public doles.

The lines which follow support this interpretation by developing the idea, inherent in the metaphorical equation of *ossa* and *lapides*, of a close bond between men and earth. In the preceding section Persius had flippantly suggested that he squander his patrimony; here he returns to his earlier emphasis on the value of land and, contrasting the barrenness of his female relatives (*sterilis*, 54) with the earth's fecundity he proposes to adopt as his heir a total stranger, Manius. He describes Manius as a *progenies terrae* (57) and *terrae filius* (59) and traces his family tree to him, alluding to the common kinship of all men stemming from their origin in the earth. A series of verbal echoes underscores the difference between Persius and his heir. The latter had complained that Persius was diminishing his inheritance (*minuas*, 37); here Persius agrees that he is (*minui*, 64), in the same proud tone with which he earlier refused to bow to old age (*minui senio*, 16). Persius, too, enjoys himself and does not worry about serving extravagant dinners (*ponere*, 23) or pleasing his heir (*accedo Bovillas*, 55), while the latter thinks only of financial accounts (*pone, accedat*, 66–67). Reiteration also contrasts Persius with the miser who indulges himself only on his birthday (*solis natalibus*, 19), and even then sprinkles his vegetables with brine and pepper himself because he fears a servant would waste these luxuries. Persius refuses to dine frugally on holidays (*festa luce*, 69), and sarcastically orders his servant to douse the cabbages with oil (68–69). Finally, the phrase *popa venter* (74), recalling *sacrum piper* (21), implies that for both the miser and the prodigal food has become a form of false religion.

In the concluding lines of the poem Persius turns from the physical hardships to the moral dangers inherent in commerce; the latter forces men to sell their souls in exchange for a greed which is never satisfied. The repetitions of *sollers* (24, 75) and *latus* (7, 76) contrast this kind of life with the peaceful existence on land advocated by Persius. On this unfinished note the Satire abruptly ends; perhaps, therefore, the author of the *Vita* is correct in his

assertion that Persius left this Satire incomplete and Cornutus removed a few verses to give it a finished appearance.[45]

[45] It is not known whether these verses belonged to the incomplete sixth
Satire or were the opening lines of a seventh. Villeneuve (1918a), p. 344,
argues in favor of the former view.

EPILOGUE

From the foregoing discussion of individual Satires we may draw some general conclusions about Persius' satiric technique. First, it should by now be evident that Persius does not speak directly in his poems but instead assumes a variety of personae. As evidence one may cite the fact that the speaker varies according to the subject of the Satire and that when Persius includes autobiographical material, as in Satires III and V, he selects details which will enhance his particular persona. Admittedly these speakers are not complex ironic masks comparable to Swift's personae, nor do they have the vividness and consistency of the protagonist of Horace's *Sermones*; rather they represent stock attitudes or points of view toward the subject matter of each poem. The persona in the prologue and Satire I, for example, tells us nothing of his personal life but instead offers a detailed analysis of his views on literature. He represents the rebellious young poet defending his own literary tradition against the Hellenizing trend of his time. Similarly in Satires II, III, and most of V, Persius impersonates three Stoic philosophers. The fact that these speakers are only slightly individualized is not as important as the fact that they argue the themes of these Satires along conventional Stoic lines. Again in Satire IV, when he abandons the first person singular persona for the obvious role of Socrates, Persius does not attempt to portray the historical Socrates but instead recreates his highly individual manner of argument characterized by irony and indirection. Even in Satires V and VI, where Persius seems to speak in his own person, closer examination reveals him in the roles of the grateful young Stoic and Horace, the advocate of moderate enjoyment. Although we may decide that Persius is not as successful as Horace in his handling of this device, we ought to recognize that he uses a persona and no longer automatically identify him with the speaker in his Satires.

The difference in the type of persona chosen by Horace and

Persius perhaps originates in their different views of satire. To make his reader more receptive to criticism Horace conceives of his satire as a friendly conversation between himself and the reader; for this reason, and because he wishes to keep his criticism indirect, Horace makes his persona the focal point of his satire and develops this speaker in great detail. Furthermore, he seldom attacks the reader directly, preferring instead to find fault with himself or with mankind in general and let the reader draw his own conclusions. Persius, on the other hand, is convinced that the evils of his society require harsher treatment and he attempts to force the reader to acknowledge his faults. To accomplish this he merely hints at his own persona and directs the reader's attention to the adversary. Then by a series of rhetorical maneuvers he skillfully draws the reader into the poem and encourages him to identify himself with the adversary. As part of this technique Persius usually emphasizes the fictional quality of the adversary to allay the reader's suspicion and he frequently leaves the reader in doubt as to whom he is criticizing. Significantly, the one Satire which does not illustrate this technique and in which the adversary is the weakest, the sixth, is also Persius' only attempt to imitate Horace.

In addition to the persona, Persius' poetic technique includes the frequent use of verbal repetition, relevant detail, and significant allusions to other writers. A concordance to the Satires would undoubtedly reveal a relatively small vocabulary and correspondingly large number of verbal repetitions in proportion to the total of 664 lines. Depending on the context of the repetition, this device may emphasize subsidiary themes, relate disparate concepts, or contrast positive and negative values. Since it is primarily an aural device, it also unites the separate sections of the poem and probably was more immediately noticeable to the Roman audience than to the modern reader. In regard to Persius' use of relevant detail, we have often seen a specific reference provide the clue to the meaning of a difficult passage. It is particularly useful to examine the literal, technical, and connotative meanings of words since even the attentive reader is likely to miss the significance of such terms as *largitor* (*prol.*, 10), *caprificus* (I.25), *caudam* (IV.15) and *ocima* (IV.22) if he does not ask himself what these words meant to Persius' audience and what relevance they have to the Satire as a whole. Equally important are the numerous echoes of other writers in Persius' work. Earlier critics sometimes cited these allusions as proof that Persius lacked originality, but since the benefits of this technique have been demonstrated in a poem like *The Waste Land,* we must re-evaluate its use in Persius' Satires. Besides the many references to Horace, Persius also recalls specific passages in Lucilius, Lucretius, and Cicero; comparison of the original context of these passages and their satiric context often adds new insight into Persius' meaning.

Another distinctive aspect of Persius' technique is the way in which he uses imagery and metaphor to unify his Satires. In Satire I the dominant metaphor translates the theme of the Satire, that style makes the man, literally, by equating the effeminate contemporary poets with their enervated poems. The subsidiary images elaborate this metaphor, endowing poetry with physical qualities by comparing it to food and sexual stimuli. In Satire III the controlling metaphor identifies the healthy man with the sane man while the subsidiary images contrast softness, pliancy, and gluttony with firmness, self-discipline, and simple eating habits. In Satire IV a series of sexual images related to exhibitionism, buying, and selling complement the dominant metaphor of the politician as a male prostitute, while in Satire V, where the freedman enslaved to his passions is equated with the true slave, the subordinate imagery concerns internal and external forms of restraint.

In each of these Satires the imagery is closely integrated with, and illuminates, the controlling metaphor. The other two Satires, II and VI, perhaps illustrate an earlier stage of this technique. The imagery in Satire II contrasts a series of positive and negative values: frankness and secrecy, internal and external cleanliness, and piety and materialism. These contrasts are interrelated inasmuch as they each express a discrepancy between appearance and reality, but they lack a unifying metaphor. In Satire VI the metaphor is present but it is not completely integrated with the rest of the imagery in the Satire. As a result the major images contrasting land and sea, country and city, and native products with foreign imports are only indirectly related to this dominant metaphor of the banquet of life and the food imagery which it inspires. Comparison of the Satires thus suggests that Persius learned gradually to organize his ideas around a controlling metaphor and a pattern of closely related subordinate images.

This last observation raises the difficult problem of the order in which the Satires were written. I do not believe that it is necessary to establish absolute, or even relative, dates for the Satires, but a case could be made for the sequence VI, II, III, IV, V, I, and the

prologue on the assumption that as a poet gains experience he becomes more proficient in handling the techniques of poetry. This
assumption is more justifiable in the case of Persius, who died at
the age of twenty-eight, when he was just starting to mature, than
it is in the case of a writer whose career extends into old age. According to this sequence Persius began his career by imitating
Horace and adopted his device of the controlling metaphor. In his
first two poems he combines this device with a series of abstract
contrasts, but gradually he assigns greater importance to the metaphor as a unifying device and develops a pattern of imagery around
it which he reveals through verbal repetition and contrast. He also
experiments with several philosophic personae in Satires II, III,
IV, and V and eventually returns to the first person in Satire I
and the prologue; this time, however, he represents himself rather
than imitating Horace. In the early poems, also, these personae
often overpower their adversaries and alienate the reader with their
severity, while in the later poems they become more tolerant and
the adversary assumes a greater role in the dialogue. Finally, in
Satire I Persius presents a laughing, witty persona, vivid dialogue,
and an interesting, vocal adversary.

Persius is certainly not an easy Latin poet, but neither is he as
difficult as many readers contend. All too often he has suffered from
unfair comparison with Horace and Juvenal with the result that
the merits of his particular type of satire are overlooked and his
talent as a serious poet ignored. Perhaps it is time to reconsider
the traditional judgment of his Satires and to reevaluate his poetic
achievement.

THE *SOKRATIKOI LOGOI*

Much of our knowledge of the Socratic literature concerning Alcibiades' political aspirations comes from the pseudo-Platonic dialogue, the *Alcibiades I,* a conversation preserved in Xenophon's *Memorabilia,* IV.2, and several fragments of Aischines' *Alcibiades.* The *Alcibiades I* is a much longer work than the conversation between Socrates and Euthydemus (here substituted for Alcibiades) presented by Xenophon, but the two works are similar in structure.[1] Both Euthydemus and Alcibiades are described as handsome young aristocrats convinced that they know, without having been taught, the nature of justice and goodness, and confident of their ability to advise the Athenians (*Mem.,* 1, 3; *Alc.,* 104a–c, 105a–d).[2] Socrates converses with each a few days before his appearance in the Assembly and proves to him that he does not know the difference between justice and injustice or good and evil (*Mem.,* 12–20; *Alc.,* 109b–113b, 115a–116d). In each dialogue Socrates alludes to the maxim "Know thyself" (*gnōthi sauton*), and soon afterward Alcibiades and Euthydemus request his help in gaining self-knowledge (*Mem.,* 24, 30; *Alc.,* 124a–b). Socrates also uses the craftsmen (*dēmiourgoi*) as examples of men who despite their technical skill

[1] Dittmar, pp. 130–144, compares these two dialogues in detail. Although in classical times the *Alcibiades I* was unquestioningly attributed to Plato, several modern scholars have been inclined to doubt its authenticity. Paul Friedländer, *Platon* (2nd ed., Berlin, 1957) 2: pp. 317–320, gives some of the more recent bibliography on the problem, to which should be added A. Motte, "Pour l'authenticité du 'Premier Alcibiade'," *l'Ant. class.* 30 (1961): pp. 5–32. Hereafter in citing parallel passages in these two dialogues, I have used the following abbreviations: *Mem.* = *Memorabilia,* IV.2 and *Alc.* = *Alcibiades I.*

[2] Dittmar, pp. 145–148, examines the reasons behind the conflicting portraits of Alcibiades in the *Alcibiades I,* one meek and one arrogant.

lack self-knowledge and are therefore comparable to slaves, and he warns both youths to avoid this kind of slavery (*Mem.*, 22–23; *Alc.*, 131a, 135c–d).[3] Upon perceiving their ignorance Alcibiades and Euthydemus are overcome with remorse and resolve to stay close to Socrates, never leaving his side (*Mem.*, 39–40; *Alc.*, 127d, cf. 118b, 135d).[4]

Aside from a few mutilated fragments in a second century A.D. papyrus, most of the remains of Aischines' *Alcibiades* are preserved in two speeches of Aelius Aristides, *On Rhetoric* and *On The Four*.[5] These fragments, which Dittmar conjectures come from the last half of the dialogue, contain Socrates' analysis of Themistocles. Alcibiades admires Themistocles but Socrates proves to him that the latter's technical knowledge (*epistēmē*), great as it was, did not prevent his eventual downfall. Apparently in Socrates' opinion Themistocles lacked something which Dittmar suggests was full *aretē*, moral and intellectual. Furthermore, since Socrates attributes Themistocles' success to his *epistēmē* rather than to chance (*tychē*), Dittmar is probably correct in assuming that Alcibiades had cited Themistocles as an example of a natural born statesman. Upon realizing that Themistocles is not the perfect leader he supposed him to be, and perceiving his own inferiority, Alcibiades weeps.[6]

Several of the themes in these fragments reappear in the Euthydemus dialogue and the *Alcibiades I*. First, as Dittmar notes, the example of Themistocles parallels that of the Persians in the *Alcibiades I*: both figures serve by comparison to persuade Alcibiades of his own insignificance.[7] Similarly, in the *Memorabilia*, IV.2.2, Socrates again emphasizes that Themistocles studied to become a successful politician. Second, the argument which these fragments

---

[3] Xenophon does not use the word *dēmiourgoi* here, but he appears to have craftsmen in mind. Cf. Dittmar, p. 125.

[4] For a discussion of this motif in Polybios, XXXI.24.12, see Paul Friedländer, "Socrates Enters Rome," *Amer. Jour. of Philol.* 66 (1945): p. 343, reprinted in his *Plato*, Bollingen Series 59 (New York, 1958) 1: p. 328.

[5] The fragments are collected in Dittmar, pp. 266–274. The papyrus is published in B. P. Grenfell and A. S. Hunt, *The Oxyrhynchus Papyri* (London, 1898–1964) 13: pp. 88–94, no. 1608. Since Dittmar's reconstruction of the beginning and end of the dialogue (pp. 97–121) is largely hypothetical, I have restricted my discussion to the fragments which are preserved.

[6] Dittmar, pp. 104–108.

[7] *Ibid.*, p. 137. Another common comparison was drawn between Cyrus and Alcibiades, e.g., in the *Cyrus* dialogues of Antisthenes; cf. Dittmar, pp. 77–84. According to Dio Chrysostom, XXI.11, these dialogues were popular as late as the first century A.D. Cf. *infra*, p. 104.

imply Alcibiades had advanced, that nature, not learning, produces statesmen, echoes the assertion in the *Alcibiades I*, 119b, that politicians are not formally educated (*apaideutoi*), and recalls Alcibiades' and Euthydemus' confidence that they know how to govern without having studied the art.[8] And, finally, Alcibiades' emotional reaction corresponds to the remorse experienced by Euthydemus (*Mem.*, 39) and Alcibiades (*Alc.*, 127d).[9]

Plato's portrait of Alcibiades in the *Symposium*, 215a–222b, offers a common source for several of these motifs.[10] There Alcibiades appears as an arrogant, self-confident youth, well aware of his physical beauty. He is superior to all but Socrates, who exercises an unusual power over him, reducing him to tears and revealing his slavish condition (215e–216a). Socrates also shows him that he neglects himself and yet presumes to advise the Athenians (216a). This last remark perhaps inspired the extensive development of the theme of caring for oneself (*epimeleia heautou*) in the *Alcibiades I* (124c ff.).

How well-known the *Alcibiades* dialogues were during the Hellenistic period is difficult to say. Two incentives existed, however, to encourage their circulation, if not widely, at least among the philosophic schools. First, several histories of philosophy and studies of the Socratics, as well as at least one life of Alcibiades, date from this period and these, in addition to using the Socratic dialogues as sources, perhaps stimulated interest in them among their readers.[11] Second, most of the philosophic schools were anxious to trace their origins back to Socrates. Among the Stoics and Cynics this ambition fostered an image of Socrates as the true *sapiens* concerned with practical ethics rather than theoretical speculation,

[8] Arguing on the analogy of the *Alcibiades I* and *Mem.*, IV.2, Dittmar suggests (pp. 108, 123–124, 126) that in the opening of Aischines' dialogue Alcibiades also prided himself on his natural endowments of beauty and rank.

[9] Gigon (1953), p. 40, calls this remorse motif "the most impressive theme of the Socrates-Alcibiades dialogues." Although in the *Alcibiades I* Alcibiades does not weep, there may be an allusion to his emotional reaction in 124d.

[10] Xenophon's portrait of Alcibiades (*Mem.*, I.2.12–48), emphasizing his cynicism, egotism, and aggressive nature, does not appear to have influenced the development of the meeker and more malleable Alcibiades.

[11] These works include two treatises entitled "On the Socratics" by Demetrius of Phaleron (b. 350 B.C.) and Idomeneus of Lampsacus (327–270 B.C., cf. Diogenes Laertius, II.20.36); a life of Alcibiades by Satyrus (third century B.C.), and one of Socrates by Hermippos of Smyrna (*ca.* 200 B.C.). On the Socratic *Nachleben* in general, see De Magalhães-Vilhena (1952b), pp. 225–230; W. Schmid and O. Stählin, *Geschichte der griechischen Literatur*, Müllers Handbuch 7, 1[8] (Munich, 1940), pp. 275–278; and Field, pp. 214–238.

content to live simply, and immune to physical and emotional stress.[12] Since Xenophon, Antisthenes, and Aischines, rather than Plato, are the major sources for this portrait of Socrates, their writings were undoubtedly popular among the Cynics and Stoics.[13]

The Stoics, through Panaetius, probably also introduced the Romans to the *Sokratikoi logoi*.[14] According to Diogenes Laertius, II.64, Panaetius established the authenticity of the Socratic dialogues of Plato, Xenophon, Antisthenes, and Aischines. Although the third-century writer does not give a source for this information, Plutarch (*Arist.*, XXVII.4) refers to a work by Panaetius entitled "Concerning Socrates" (*Peri Sokratous*), which Van Straaten suggests may have been entitled "Concerning Socrates and the Socratics" (*Peri Sokratous kai tōn Sokratikōn*), and which may have discussed the authenticity of these works.[15] In addition, Panaetius discussed the stylistic requirements of the *Sokratikoi logoi* in his treatise "On Decorum" (*Peri tou kathēkontos*), from which Cicero derives his analysis of the Socratic *sermo* in the *De officiis*, I.132–134. As a frequent visitor to Rome during the years 146–129 B.C. and a leading member of the Scipionic circle, Panaetius is the logical person to have introduced the Romans to the Socratic dialogues; and in fact Cicero may have had him in mind when he remarked:

Aut quid P. Scipione, quid C. Laelio, quid L. Philo perfectius cogitari potest? qui, ne quid praetermitterent quod ad summam laudem clarorum virorum pertineret, ad domesticorum maiorumque morem etiam hanc a Socrate adventiciam doctrinam adhibuerunt [*Rep.*, III.3.5].[16]

---

[12] A. Jagu, *Épictète et Platon* (Paris, 1946), pp. 29–33. Field, p. 215, suggests that Antisthenes may have passed on to his pupil Zeno this Cynic portrait of Socrates. For further discussion on this point, see Donald R. Dudley, *A History of Cynicism* (London, 1937), pp. 8–14 and R. Hoïstad, *Cynic Hero and Cynic King* (Uppsala, 1948), pp. 8–12.

[13] De Magalhães-Vilhena (1952b), pp. 35–36. Cf. Dudley, p. 14, Field, pp. 155–156. It is true, however, that Alcibiades also emphasizes Socrates' asceticism and powers of physical endurance in the *Symposium*, 219c–221b *passim*. In regard to the later influence of the *Sokratikoi logoi* Olof Gigon remarks (1946), p. 151: "Finally, the Socratic philosophers retain a particular importance when we consider the extent to which (even if we cannot fix limits) the Socratic *logoi* were the reservoir from which Hellenistic philosophy drew its ethical thought."

[14] K. Münscher, "Xenophon in der grieschisch-römischen Literatur," *Philologus*, Suppl. 13 (Leipzig, 1920), pp. 54–56.

[15] M. van Straaten, *Panétius, sa vie, ses écrits et sa doctrine* (Amsterdam, 1946), p. 36. Van Straaten advances this suggestion very tentatively.

[16] Pliny, *Hist. Nat.* XXXIV.26, also relates that the Romans erected a statue of Alcibiades, along with one of Pythagoras, in the Comitium [*ca.* 343 B.C.], and these statues remained standing until the time of Sulla. If true, this would imply an interest in his career. Cf. Plutarch, *Numa*, VIII.

Who can be considered more perfect than P. Scipio, C. Laelius, and L. Philo? These men, lest they overlook anything which might contribute to the high praise of outstanding men, combined the imported teachings of Socrates with the tradition of their own people and their ancestors.

Panaetius' influence has also been traced in the works of Lucilius and Polybius.[17] Although we cannot conjecture much on the basis of a single reference to the *Socratici carti* in Lucilius (Marx, ed., 709–710), Friedländer has argued convincingly that Polybius' famous conversation with Scipio Aemilianus, which he records in his history (XXXI.23–25), owes much to the *Alcibiades I*.[18] This is not surprising since Polybius was a Stoic as well as a member of the Scipionic circle but, if true, it is significant, I think, that the *Alcibiades I* was imitated in Rome as early as the second century B.C.

In the introduction to the second book of the *Tusculan Disputations* Cicero contrasts the popularity of Plato and the Socratics with that of Epicurus and his followers:

Nam ut Platonem reliquosque Socraticos et deinceps eos, qui ab his profecti sunt, legunt omnes, etiam qui illa aut non approbant aut non studiosissime consectantur, Epicurum autem et Metrodorum non fere praeter suos quisquam in manus sumit . . . [II.3.8].

While Plato and his fellow Socratics, as well as their followers, are read by everyone including those who disagree with their views or those who are not enthusiastic about philosophy, hardly anyone reads Epicurus and Metrodorus except their disciples.

This statement clearly suggests that Roman interest in the *Sokratikoi logoi* continued into the first century B.C. Cicero, we know, had read some of Antisthenes' works, and there are several references

---

[17] Puelma Piwonka, pp. 116–167 *passim*. R. v. Scala, *Die Studien des Polybios* (Stuttgart, 1890) 1: pp. 201 ff.

[18] P. Friedländer (1945), pp. 337–351. While I agree that the parallels noted by Friedländer point to a conscious imitation of the *Alcibiades I*, I believe that instead of equating Scipio with Alcibiades, Polybius intends to contrast the two youths to Scipio's advantage. In the Socratic dialogue Alcibiades is arrogant, conceited, and confident of his political ability, and it is Socrates who has been quietly following him around (103a). In contrast, Scipio is reticent and worried lest people say that he is not a credit to his family, and it is he who quietly pursues Polybius. Furthermore, every virtue attributed to Scipio is discussed in the *Alcibiades I*, and while none are characteristic of Alcibiades, several of them are Persian virtues (cf. 115b, 122a–c, 124e, 131b). Scipio too, like the Persians, has learned courage through hunting (cf. *Alc. I*, 121e, Polyb., XXIX.7–10). These similarities are significant because the superiority of the Persians is emphasized in the Greek dialogue to magnify Alcibiades' inferiority. There may also be a reminiscence of Aischines' portrait of Themistocles in Polybius' final statement that Scipio himself, rather than chance (*tychē*), was responsible for his worthy deeds (XXX.3).

to the Socratic dialogues in his writings.[19] One may certainly argue that Cicero himself describes these writings as *apographa*, "translations" (*ad Att.*, XII.52), and that it is difficult to distinguish the material of his Greek sources from his own additions. On the other hand, since Cicero was a great admirer of Plato and the self-appointed transmitter of Greek philosophy into Roman culture, it is not unlikely that he had read the better known of the *Sokratikoi logoi*, including the *Alcibiades I* and Aischines' *Alcibiades*.[20] In the *Tusculan Disputations* there are two passages which appear to reflect these dialogues. The first (I.22.52) is an obvious allusion to the *Alcibiades I* which Cicero may have found in an intermediary source,[21] but the origin of the second is more problematic. This passage occurs in the third book when Cicero, after criticizing Cleanthes for overlooking the fact that recognition of *turpitudo* often produces *aegritudo*, asks:

Quid enim dicemus, cum Socrates Alcibiadi persuassiset, ut accipimus, eum nihil hominis esse nec quicquam inter Alcibiadem summo loco natum et quemvis baiolum interesse, cum se Alcibiades adflictaret lacrimansque Socrati supplex esset, ut sibi virtutem traderet turpitudinemque depelleret, quid dicemus, Cleanthe? [III.32.77]

What shall we say when we hear that, after Socrates had persuaded Alcibiades that he was not a man at all and that there was no difference

---

[19] Cicero, *ad Att.*, XII.38: κῦρος, δ, έ *mihi sic placuit, ut cetera Antisthenis, hominis acuti magis quam eruditi* (*Cyrus* IV and V pleased me as much as the other works of Antisthenes, a man more intelligent than learned).

[20] Thelma B. DeGraff, "Plato in Cicero," *Class. Phil.* 35 (1940): pp. 143–153, gives a fairly complete list of Platonic reminiscences in Cicero, but she overlooks the allusion to the *Alcibiades I* in the *Tusc. Disp.*, I.22.52, and she does not give a source for *Tusc. Disp.*, III.32.77, except to say, p. 151, n. 81, that it is not Platonic. For a more comprehensive discussion of Plato's influence on Cicero, see Pierre Boyancé, "Le platonisme à Rome: Platon et Cicéron," *Actes du Congrès Budé de Tours et Poitiers* (Paris, 1954): pp. 195–221, and "Cicéron et le *Premier Alcibiade*," *Rev. étud. lat.* 41 (1963): pp. 210–229. In the latter article Boyancé argues that Cicero derives his interpretation of the maxim *nosce te ipsum* (*De leg.*, I.22.58, *De fin.*, V.16.44, *Tusc. Disp.*, V.25.70) ultimately from the *Alcibiades I* through Antiochus of Ascalon. Cf. also Olof Gigon, "Die Erneuerung der Philosophie in der Zeit Ciceros," *Entretiens de la Fondation Hardt* 3 (Geneva, 1955): pp. 25–61.

[21] This passage in the *Tusculan Disputations* clearly echoes the *Alcibiades I*, 130e (cf. 133b), as R. Adam, "Ueber der Echtheit und Abfassungszeit des platonischen Alcibiades I," *Archiv für Geschichte der Philosophie* 14, 7 (1901): p. 58, noted long ago. The context of the passage suggests that Cicero is following a source here which included this quote, but which source remains in doubt. For a discussion of the various possibilities, see R. M. Jones, "Posidonius and Cicero's *Tusculan Disputations* I.17–81," *Class. Phil.* 18 (1923): pp. 214–215 (not Posidonius); A. Barigazzi, "Sulle fonti del libro I delle Tusculane di Cicerone," *Riv. di filol. e d'ist. class.* 76, 26 (1948): p. 171 (Aristotle's early writings); and O. Gigon (1955), pp. 58–59 (no single philosopher).

between him, born into the upper class, and any laborer, Alcibiades threw himself down and in tears begged Socrates to teach him virtue and dispel his base habits—when we hear this, Cleanthes, what shall we say? Dittmar believes that this anecdote derives from Aischines' Alcibiades,[22] but whether or not Cicero had read this dialogue depends upon the meaning of *ut accipimus*. This phrase may mean that Cicero is here relying upon an intermediary source, but to me it suggests that he is introducing a literary anecdote rather than an historical incident and one, furthermore, which is found in several authors and has become part of the Alcibiades tradition. As we have seen, this is true of the motif of Alcibiades weeping, so perhaps Aischines' dialogue is one of the works referred to in the phrase *ut accipimus*.[23]

The same problem confronts us when we try to evaluate Horace's references to the Socratic dialogues. The well-known precept in the *Ars Poetica*,

[22] Cf. the fragment of Aischines preserved in Aelius Aristides, *On the Four*, 285 (Dittmar, pp. 271–272):

καὶ οὗ κακῶς λέγει τὸν Θεμιστοκλέα παρόντος ἐκείνου, ὅπως μὴ ἔτι μᾶλλον ἀκούων διαφθείροιτο, οὐδέ γε εἰς παραμυθίας μέρος αὐτῷ κατατίθεται τὸ μὴ μόνον αὐτὸν τῇ ἀμαθίᾳ συνοικεῖν, ἀλλὰ καὶ πάντας εἶναι τοιούτους, ὅσοι τὰ τῆς πόλεως πράττουσιν. οὐδαμῶς. ἀλλ' ἀναγκάζει "κλάειν θέντα τὴν κεφαλὴν ἐπὶ τὰ γόνατα ἀθυμήσαντα, ὡς οὐδ' ἐγγὺς ὄντα τῷ Θεμιστοκλεῖ τὴν παρασκευήν."

[Socrates] wisely speaks of Themistocles when Alcibiades is present, so that by listening a little longer he may avoid corruption. Socrates does not console Alcibiades, however, with the thought that he is not the only one to dwell in ignorance but that this is characteristic of all who manage the affairs of the city—certainly not; rather he compels him "to weep, his head on his knees, completely disheartened because he has nowhere near the ability of Themistocles."

Dittmar, p. 99, n. 14, following Pohlenz, assumes that this scene is ultimately the source of Cicero's anecdote because here it is the recognition of his inferiority which leads Alcibiades to weep. Before Dittmar, F. A. Wolf, *Ciceronis Tusculanarum Disputationum Libri V*, ed. Orelli (Zurich, 1829 n.v.), had conjectured that this anecdote occurred in a lost Socratic dialogue and Orelli, *ibid.*, excluded the *Symposium*, 215e as a source, "since the words *quemvis baiolum* give a strong individual character to the narrative, which appears to have been literally translated from some Greek original (quoted from T. W. Dougan and R. M. Henry, *M. Tulli Ciceronis Tusculanarum Disputationum Libri Quinque* [Cambridge, 1934] 2: p. 96). It should also be pointed out that in the *Symposium*, 215e there is no comparison with a *dēmiourgos*. Aelius Aristides, it is true, does not mention any such comparison, but since he only summarizes the scene here, his words do not exclude the possibility of such a comparison. In lieu of evidence to the contrary, Dittmar's identification of Aischines as a source for this anecdote is at least possible.

[23] It seems unlikely to me that Cicero followed his Greek sources so closely as to translate every adverbial phrase verbatim. *Ut accipimus* appears to be one of Cicero's characteristic attempts to play down his first-hand knowledge of Greek literature.

Scribendi recte sapere est et principium
et fons:
rem tibi Socraticae potuerunt ostendere
chartae,
verbaque provisam rem non invita sequentur . . . [309–311].

Wisdom is the principal source of the art of writing well. The Socratic
tracts can show you your subject matter and the words will follow of
their own accord,

implies but does not necessarily prove that Horace had read these
treatises because, as C. O. Brink points out, this is also an important
doctrine of Neoptolemus, Horace's source in this poem.[24] Horace
would hardly have recommended that his audience read these
dialogues, however, if they were not available in Rome and he
were not familiar with them. In one of his odes, moreover, Horace
says of his friend Corvinus, *Socraticis madit / sermonibus* (he is
steeped in the Socratic dialogues, III.21.9–10), and in another he
chides Iccius for exchanging *libros Panaeti Socraticam et domum* (the
works of Panaetius and the Socratic camp), for a military expedition
to Arabia (I.29.14). These remarks suggest that Horace and his
educated friends still studied the Socratics.

The increasing influence of the Stoics and Cynics in Rome during
the first century A.D. undoubtedly explains the upsurge of interest
in the *Sokratikoi logoi* at this time. Persius is not the only author
in this period to use Alcibiades as a character; according to Dio
Chrysostom (XXI.11) the Cyrus-Alcibiades dialogues were popular
with the *sophoi*, whom Hoïstad identifies with the Cynics.[25] In
addition, the Cynic-Stoic Socrates is a familiar figure in Epictetus'
Discourses and in one which resembles Persius' fourth Satire,
Epictetus quotes the *Alcibiades I* from memory.[26] Several other
passages also contain reminiscences of this dialogue.[27] This evidence
is particularly important because Epictetus lectured in Rome during
the late first century A.D. and like Persius he was a doctrinaire
Stoic, a follower of Chrysippus and Cleanthes rather than Panaetius
and Posidonius.[28] His writings reflect the academic Stoicism which

---

[24] C. O. Brink, *Horace on Poetry* (Cambridge, 1963), pp. 129–131. Propertius,
II.34.25–28 also alludes to the *Socraticis libris* as if the phrase was an eponym
for moral philosophy in general. On the other hand, W. S. Anderson (1963)
argues that Horace's satiric persona is carefully modeled after Socrates, which,
if true, suggests a thorough acquaintance with the *Socraticae chartae*.
[25] Hoïstad, p. 89.
[26] Epictetus, *Diss.*, III.1.42 (cf. *Alc. I*, 131d).
[27] Jagu, p. 138, n. 1–10, gives a complete list.
[28] *Ibid.*, p. 154.

Persius also studied, and the importance of Socrates in his writings suggests that the Socratic dialogues were an important part of the Stoic curriculum and that Persius' study of these dialogues may have prompted him to write the fourth Satire.

BIBLIOGRAPHY

Adam, R. 1901. "Ueber der Echtheit und Abfassungszeit des platonischen Alcibiades I." *Archiv für Geschichte der Philosophie* 14, 7: pp. 40–65.

Aden, John. 1962. "Pope and the Satiric Adversary." *Studies in English Literature* 2: pp. 267–286.

Adolf, King Gustaf of Sweden, and Axel Boethius. 1963. *Etruscan Culture, Land, and People* (New York).

Allen, Archibald W. 1950. " 'Sincerity' and the Roman Elegists." *Classical Philology* 45: pp. 145–160.

Anderson, William S. 1958. "Persius 1. 107–110." *Classical Quarterly* 58: pp. 195–197.

—————.1960a. "Imagery in the Satires of Horace and Juvenal." *American Journal of Philology* 81: pp. 225–260.

—————. 1960b. "Part Versus Whole in Persius' Fifth Satire." *Philological Quarterly* 39: pp. 66–81.

—————. 1961. "Juvenal and Quintilian." *Yale Classical Studies* 17: pp. 3–93.

—————. 1963. "The Roman Socrates: Horace and His Satires." *Critical Essays on Roman Literature,* ed. J. P. Sullivan (2 v., London) 2: pp. 1–37.

—————. 1964a. "Anger in Juvenal and Seneca." *University of California Publications in Classical Philology* 19, 3: pp. 127–196.

—————. 1964b. "Roman Satirists and Literary Criticism." *Bucknell Review* 12: pp. 106–113.

————— *et al.* 1966. Symposium: "The Concept of the Persona in Satire." *Satire Newsletter* 3: pp. 89–153.

Aristotle. 1886. *Aristotelis qui ferebantur librorum fragmenta,* ed. V. Rose (Leipzig).

—————. 1877. *The Rhetoric,* ed. E. M. Cope and J. E. Sandys (3 v., Cambridge).

Bardon, H. 1936. "Les poésies de Néron." *Revue des études latines* 14: pp. 337–349.

—————. 1940. *Les Empereurs et les lettres latines d'Auguste à Hadrien* (Paris).

Barigazzi, A. 1948, 1950. "Sulle fonti del libro I delle Tusculane di Cicerone." *Rivista di filologia e d'istruzione classica* 76, 26: pp. 161–203; 78, 28: pp. 1–29.

Boyancé, Pierre. 1954. "Le platonisme à Rome. Platon et Cicéron." *Actes du Congrès Budé de Tours et Poitiers* (Paris), pp. 195–221.

———. 1963. "Cicéron et le *Premier Alcibiade.*" *Revue des études latines* 41: pp. 210–229.

Brink, C. O. 1963. *Horace on Poetry* (Cambridge).

Bücheler, F. 1871. "Zur höfischen Poesie unter Nero." *Rheinisches Museum* 26: pp. 235–240, reprinted in his *Kleine Schriften* (2 v., Leipzig/Berlin, 1927) 2: pp. 1–6.

Burnier, Charles. 1909. *Le Rôle des satires de Perse dans le développement du néo-stoïcisme* (Chaux-de-Fonds).

Cartault, André. 1921a. "Les Choliambes de Perse." *Revue de philologie* 45: pp. 63–65.

———. 1921b. "La Satire I de Perse." *Revue de philologie* 45: pp. 66–74.

Cherniss, Harold. 1933–1944. "The Biographical Fashion in Literary Criticism." *University of California Publications in Classical Philology* 12: pp. 279–291.

Ciaffi, Vincenzo. 1942. *Introduzione a Persio* (Turin).

Cicero. 1934. *Tusculanarum Disputationum Libri Quinque*, ed. T. W. Dougan and R. M. Henry (2 v., Cambridge).

Ciresola, T. 1953. *La formazione del linguaggio poetico di Persio* (Rovereto).

Clausen, Wendell V. 1963. "Sabinus' MS of Persius." *Hermes* 91: pp. 252–256.

Courcelle, Pierre. 1955. "Histoire du cliché virgilien des cent bouches." *Revue des études latines* 33: pp. 231–240.

d'Agostino, V. 1929. "La seconda satira di Persio e 'l'auri sacra fames'." *Convivium* 1: pp. 573–579.

d'Alton, John F. 1962. *Roman Literary Theory and Criticism* (repr., New York).

d'Anna, Giovanni. 1964. "Persio *semipaganus.*" *Rivista di cultura classica e medioevale* 6: pp. 181–185.

Dawson, Christopher. 1950. "The Iambi of Callimachus." *Yale Classical Studies* 11: pp. 1–149.

DeGraff, Thelma B. 1940. "Plato in Cicero." *Classical Philology* 35: pp. 143–153.

De Lacy, Philip. 1948. "Stoic Views of Poetry." *American Journal of Philology* 69: pp. 241–271.

Desmouliez, André. 1955. "La Signification esthétique des comparaisons entre le style et le corps humain dans la rhétorique antique." *Revue des études latines* 33: p. 59.

Dittmar, Heinrich. 1912. *Aischines von Sphettos*, Philologische Untersuchungen, 21 (Berlin).

Dryden, John. 1963. "A Discourse Concerning the Original and Progress of Satire." *Essays of John Dryden*, ed. W. P. Ker (2 v., repr. New York, 1961) 2: pp. 15–114.

Dudley, Donald R. 1937. *A History of Cynicism* (London).

Duff, J. W. 1960. *A Literary History of Rome in the Silver Age* (2nd ed., London).

Durling, Robert M. 1957–1958. "Ovid as *Praeceptor Amoris.*" *Classical Journal* 53: pp. 157–167.

———. 1965. *The Figure of the Poet in Renaissance Epic* (Cambridge).

Ehrenpreis, Irvin. 1963. "Personae." *Restoration and Eighteenth Century Literature: Essays in Honor of Alan Dugald McKillop,* ed. C. Camden (Chicago), pp. 25–37.

Ennius. 1903. *Ennianae Poesis Reliquiae,* ed. I. Vahlen (Leipzig).

Ewald, W. B. 1954. *The Masks of Jonathan Swift* (Oxford).

Faranda, G. 1955. "Caratteristiche dello stile e del linguaggio poetico di Persio." *Rendiconti del Istituto Lombardo,* Cl. di Lett. 88: pp. 512–538.

Festa, Nicola. 1936. "Persio e Cleante." *Scritti per il XIX centenario dalla nascità di Persio* (Volterra), pp. 15–30.

Field, George C. 1930. *Plato and His Contemporaries* (London).

Fiske, G. C. 1920. *Lucilius and Horace,* University of Wisconsin Studies in Language and Literature 7 (Madison).

Frank, Tenney. 1940. *An Economic Survey of Ancient Rome* (5 v., Baltimore).

Friedländer, Ludwig. 1913. *Roman Life and Manners Under the Early Empire* (4 v., London).

Friedländer, Paul. 1945. "Socrates Enters Rome." *American Journal of Philology* 66: pp. 337–351, reprinted in his *Plato,* tr. Meyerhoff, Bollingen Series 59 (2 v., New York, 1958) 1: pp. 323–332.

———. 1957. *Platon* (2 v., 2nd ed., Berlin).

Gaar, E. 1909–1910a. "Persiusprobleme." *Wiener Studien* 31–32: pp. 128–135, 233–243.

———. 1909–1910b. "Persius und Lucilius." *Wiener Studien* 31–32: pp. 244–249.

Gerhard, G. 1913. "Der Prolog des Persius." *Philologus* 72: pp. 484–491.

Gigon, Olof. 1946. "Xenophontea." *Eranos Rudbergianus* 44: pp. 131–152.

———. 1953. *Kommentar zum ersten Buch von Xenophons Memorabilien,* Schweizerische Beiträge zur Altertumswissenschaft, 5 (Basel).

———. 1955. "Die Erneuerung der Philosophie in der Zeit Ciceros." *Entretiens de la Fondation Hardt* (Geneva) 3: pp. 25–61.

Grenfell, B. P., and A. S. Hunt. 1898–1964. *The Oxyrhynchus Papyri* (30 v., London).

Griset, E. 1954. " 'LUNAI PORTUM' o 'lunai portum'." *Rivista di studi classici* 2: pp. 13–16.

Halliday, W. R. 1924. "Persius, II.37." *Classical Review* 38: p. 169.

Hendrickson, George. 1928a. "The First Satire of Persius." *Classical Philology* 23: pp. 97–112.

———. 1928b. "The Third Satire of Persius." *Classical Philology* 23: pp. 332–342.

Henss, D. 1955. "Die Imitationstechnik des Persius." *Philologus* 99: pp. 277–294.

Hirzel, Rudolf. 1895. *Der Dialog* (2 v., Leipzig).

Hoïstad, R. 1948. *Cynic Hero and Cynic King* (Uppsala).

Holloway, John. 1956. "The Well-Filled Dish: An Analysis of Swift's Satire." *Hudson Review* 9: pp. 20–37.

Housman, Alfred E. 1913. "Notes on Persius." *Classical Quarterly* 7: pp. 12–32.

——. 1934. "Ennius in Pers. VI.9." *Classical Review* 48: pp. 50–51.

Jagu, Amand. 1946. *Épictète et Platon* (Paris).

Jones, R. M. 1923. "Posidonius and Cicero's *Tusculan Disputations* I.17–81." *Classical Philology* 18: pp. 202–228.

Keil, H., ed. 1857–1880. *Grammatici Latini* (7 v., Leipzig).

Kennedy, George. 1962. "An Estimate of Quintilian." *American Journal of Philology* 83: pp. 130–146.

Kernan, Alvin. 1959. *The Cankered Muse: Satire of the English Renaissance* (New Haven).

Kugler, Wolfgang. 1940. *Des Persius' Wille zu sprachlicher Gestaltung in seiner Wirkung auf Ausdruck und Komposition* (Diss., Berlin/Wurzburg).

Lackenbacher, H. 1937. "Persius und die Heilkunde." *Wiener Studien* 55: pp. 130–141.

Leo, F. 1910. "Zum Text des Persius und Iuvenal." *Hermes* 45: pp. 43–56.

Leumann, M., J. Hofmann, and A. Szantyr. 1963–1965. *Lateinische Grammatik,* Müllers Handbuch, II, 2$^{1-2}$ (2 v., Munich).

Levi, M. A. 1949. *Nerone e i suoi tempi* (Milan).

Longinus. 1960. *On the Sublime,* tr. W. Hamilton Fyfe (Cambridge).

Lucilius. 1904–1905. *Carminum Reliquiae,* ed. Marx (2 v., Leipzig).

Lucretius. 1950. *De rerum natura libri sex,* ed. C. Bailey (repr., 3 v., Oxford).

McGann, M. J. 1954. "Horace's Epistle to Florus (Epist. 2.2)." *Rheinisches Museum* 97: pp. 343–358.

Mack, Maynard. 1951. "The Muse of Satire." *Yale Review* 41: pp. 80–92.

Mackey, Louis. 1965. "Aristotle and Feidelson on Metaphor: Toward a Reconciliation of Ancient and Modern." *Arion* 4, 2: pp. 272–285.

Magalhães-Vilhena, V. de. 1952a. *Le Problème de Socrate* (Paris).

——. 1952b. *Socrate et la légende platonicienne* (Paris).

Manitius, M. 1888. "Beiträge zur Geschichte römischer Dichter im Mittelalter." *Philologus* 47: pp. 710–720.

——. 1892. "Philologisches aus alten Bibliothekskatalogen (bis 1300)." *Rheinisches Museum* 47, Supplementbd.

Marache, R. 1952. *La Critique littéraire de langue latine et le développement du goût archaïsant au IIe siècle de notre ère* (Rennes).

Marmorale, Enzo. 1956. *Persio* (2nd ed., Florence).

Martin, J. 1939. "Persius, Poet of the Stoics." *Greece and Rome* 8: pp. 172–182.

Merone, E. 1954. "L'infinito aoristico in Persio." *Giornale italiano di filologia* 7: pp. 244–255.

Motte, A. 1961. "Pour l'authenticité du 'Premier Alcibiade'." *L'Antiquité classique* 30: pp. 5–32.

Münscher, K. 1920. "Xenophon in der grieschisch-römischen Literatur." *Philologus, Supplementbd.* 13 (Leipzig), pp. 1–236.

Otto, A. 1890. *Die Sprichwörter und sprichwörtlichen Redensarten der Römer* (Leipzig).

Paratore, E. 1951. *Storia della letteratura latina* (Florence).

Pareti, L. 1918–1919. "Portus Lunae." *Atene e Roma* 21–22: pp. 131–158.

Paulson, Ronald. 1960. Review of Alvin Kernan, *The Cankered Muse.* *Journal of English and Germanic Philology* 59: pp. 737–740.

Persius. 1605. *Auli Persi Flacci Saturarum Liber,* ed. Isaac Casaubon (Paris).

———. 1752. *The Satyrs of Persius,* tr. E. Burton (London).

———. 1843. *Auli Persii Flacci Satirarum Liber cum scholiis antiquis,* ed. Otto Jahn (Leipzig).

———. 1875. *The Satires of A. Persius Flaccus,* ed. Basil Gildersleeve (New York).

———. 1893. *The Satires of A. Persius Flaccus,* ed. J. Conington and Henry Nettleship (3rd ed., Oxford).

———. 1903. *A. Persii Flacci Satirae,* ed. Geyza Némethy (Budapest).

———. 1907. *A. Persii Flacci Saturarum Liber,* ed. G. Albini (Imola).

———. 1949. *A. Persi Flacci et D. Iuni Iuvenalis Saturae,* ed. S. G. Owen (2nd ed., Oxford).

———. 1956. *A. Persi Flacci Saturarum Liber,* ed. Wendell V. Clausen (Oxford).

———. 1956. *Auli Persi Flacci Saturae,* ed. Nino Scivoletto (Florence).

———. 1961. *The Satires of Persius,* tr. W. S. Merwin (Bloomington).

Pierruges, P. 1826. *Glossarium Eroticum Linguae Latinae* (Paris).

Piwonka, Mario Puelma. 1949. *Lucilius und Kallimachos* (Frankfurt).

Pretor, Alfred. 1907. "A Few Notes on the *Satires* of Persius with Special Reference to the Purport and Position of the Prologue." *Classical Review* 21: pp. 72–74.

Rambelli, G. 1957. "I coliambi di Persio." *Studi di filologia classica* (Pavia), pp. 3–8.

Randolph, Mary C. 1939. *The Neo-Classic Theory of the Formal Verse Satire in England, 1700–1750* (Diss., University of North Carolina).

———. 1942. "The Structural Design of the Formal Verse Satire." *Philological Quarterly* 21: pp. 368–384.

Reckford, Kenneth J. 1962. "Studies in Persius." *Hermes* 90: pp. 476–504.

Reitzenstein, R. 1924. "Zur römischen Satire: zu Persius und Lucilius." *Hermes* 59: pp. 1–22.

Rose, H. J. 1924. "Some Traps in Persius' First Satire." *Classical Review* 38: pp. 63–64.

Rostagni, A. 1944. *Suetonio de Poetis e biografi minori* (Turin).

Rudd, Niall. 1964. "The Style and the Man." *Phoenix* 18: pp. 216–231.

———. 1966. *The Satires of Horace* (Cambridge).

Scala, R. v. 1890. *Die Studien des Polybios* (2 v., Stuttgart).

Scaliger, Julius C. 1561. *Poetices Libri Septem* (Lyon).

Scarcia, Riccardo. 1964. "Osservazioni critiche." *Rivista di cultura classica e medioevale* 6: pp. 287–302.

Schanz, M., and C. Hosius. 1935. *Geschichte der römischen Literatur,* Müllers Handbuch, 8, 2^2 (4th ed., Munich).

Schmid, W., and O. Stählin. 1940. *Geschichte der griechischen Literatur,* Müllers Handbuch, 7, 1^3 (Munich).

Seel, O. 1960. Review of Wendell Clausen, ed., *A. Persi Flacci Saturarum Liber. Gnomon* 32: pp. 119–128.

Shero, Lucius. 1922. "The Satirist's Apologia." *University of Wisconsin Studies in Language and Literature* 15: pp. 148–167.

Spaeth, J. W. 1942. "Persius on Epicurus: A Note on *Satires* 3.83–84." *Transactions of the American Philological Association* 73: pp. 119–122.

Stanford, W. B. 1936. *Greek Metaphor* (Oxford).

Straaten, M. van. 1946. *Panétius, sa vie, ses écrits, et sa doctrine* (Amsterdam).

Syme, Ronald. 1958. *Tacitus* (2 v., Oxford).

Terzaghi, Nicola. 1936. "La terza satira di Persio." *Scritti per il XIX centenario dalla nascità di Persio* (Volterra), pp. 85–97.

———. 1943. "Satira e poesia nella letteratura latina." *Annali della scuola normale superiore di Pisa*, Cl. di lett. 12: pp. 99–110.

———. 1944. *Per la storia della satira* (2nd ed., Messina).

Thomas, Paul. 1920. "Notes critiques et explicatives sur les "Satires" de Perse." *Bulletin de l'académie royale de Belgique*, Cl. des lett., pp. 45–66.

Tibullus. 1913. *The Elegies*, ed. Kirby F. Smith (New York).

Van Hook, Larue. 1905. *The Metaphorical Terminology of Greek Rhetoric and Literary Criticism* (Diss., University of Chicago).

Verdière, R. 1956. "Notes critiques sur Perse." *Collection Latomus* 23: pp. 339–350.

Villeneuve, Francois. 1918a. *Essai sur Perse* (Paris).

———. 1918b. *Les Satires de Perse* (Paris).

Waszink, J. H. 1943. "Varia critica et exegetica." *Mnemosyne* 3, 11: pp. 68–77.

———. 1950. "The Proem of the Annales of Ennius." *Mnemosyne* 4, 3: pp. 214–240.

———. 1962. "Retractio Enniana." *Mnemosyne* 4, 15: pp. 113–132.

Weinreich, Otto. 1928. *Studien zu Martial* (Stuttgart).

West, M. L. 1961. "Persius i. 1–3." *Classical Review* 11: p. 204.

Wilamowitz-Moellendorff, Ulrich von. 1920. *Platon* (2 v., 2nd ed., Berlin).

Williams, Kathleen. 1961. Review of Alvin Kernan, *The Cankered Muse. Modern Language Notes* 76: pp. 346–348.

Wimmel, W. 1960. *Kallimachos in Rom*, Hermes Einzelschriften, 16 (Wiesbaden).

Witke, Edward C. 1961. *Latin Satire: The Classical Genre and Its Medieval Development* (Diss., Harvard University).

———. 1962. "The Function of Persius' Choliambics." *Mnemosyne* 4, 15: pp. 153–158.

Womble, Hilburn. 1961. "Repetition and Irony: Horace, *Odes* 2.18." *Transactions of the American Philological Association* 92: pp. 537–549.

INDEX

DATE DUE
